A Handbook of Creative Dance and Drama.

Alison Lee

HEINEMANN Portsmouth, NH

Heinemann Educational Books, Inc.
361 Hanover Street
Portsmouth, NH 03801–3959
Offices and agents throughout the world.

Copyright © Alison Lee 1985
First published 1985 by Longman Cheshire Pty Limited, Melbourne, Australia.
First published in United States of America 1991
by Heinemann Educational Books.

Designed by Noniann Cabouret Lier
Illustrated by Rebecca Panell

Printed in Malaysia
Sun U Book Co. Sdn. Bhd., Kuala Lumpur.

Lee, Alison, 1950–
    A handbook of creative dance and drama/Alison Lee.
        p.   cm.
    Originally published: Melbourne, Australia: Longman Cheshire,
    1985.
    ISBN 0–435–08702–9

    1. Movement education. 2. Dancing for children — Study and
    teaching (Elementary) 3. Drama — Study and teaching (Elementary)
    4. Drama in education. I. Title.
GV452.L44 1991   91–4980
372.86 — dc20   CIP

contents

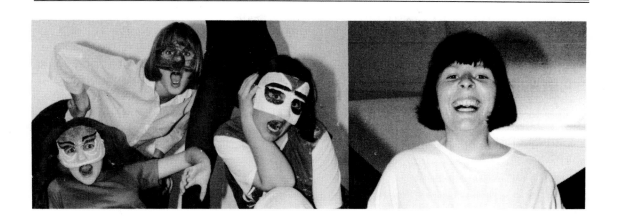

chapter 1:   how to use this book

Introduction

1   **The use of this handbook** will vary from person to person. For some, it might be the first time they have used creative dance and drama in the classroom; for others, it could augment an existing programme; and some might wish to specialise in a particular area, such as mask work or pure dance.

2   **The exercises** have been tried and tested with a number of children in different schools and age groups. I have worked in schools for a number of years and the book is based on my practical experience both as a teacher and as a pupil.

3   **The age range** for the activities is from Kindergarten to Year 6, but in some cases I have mentioned that I have found a specific exercise particularly useful with a certain age group. It is up to you to choose exercises, language, concepts and movements suitable for your children. If you like the idea of an exercise, but think it is too easy or difficult for your class, then modify it accordingly.

4   **The book is intended mainly as a foundation** on which to build creative movement work, not as a gospel. Adapt and build on the ideas and activities.

5   **Fun** is the active ingredient in all creative movement work. Children are motivated by fun to explore themselves and the environment, to communicate with others and to gain a positive and creative self concept. Through imagination, observation, co-ordination and creative activity, a human being can control his environment.

6   **The attitude of the teacher** is most important, as it will influence the class. If you are prepared to join in, demonstrate and enter into the fantasies, the children will respond.

7   **A comfortable atmosphere** is needed for children to be able to work without feeling inhibited by the teacher's or other children's judgements. (That is why many exercises are done individually.) If the children feel too competitive they will try to please the teacher or 'be the best', rather than experiencing the exercise for its own sake. I often refrain from verbal comment altogether, but note what is happening and step in to create an exercise to develop a certain skill if necessary.

8   **Performance**. Audiences can range from other members of the class to 1000 strangers at a music festival. Performance, if handled properly, is a great opportunity for children to develop skills and confidence.

    Classroom and school performances are a good testing ground, especially classroom performances in which you can create a safe atmosphere. The watching children are encouraged to respect the performer as a person, and for his/her courage in standing up there in front of classmates. I allow no disrespectful behaviour during a performance, and the idea quickly catches on when all the children realise that their turn up front will come.

    Public performances must be of high quality. You are responsible for seeing that the children go on stage adequately rehearsed, confident and with a performance piece they enjoy sharing with others. I choose pieces in which the natural joy, beauty and liveliness of the children come through. These attributes are polished by good technique, costumes and an exciting story or theme. The children are encouraged to look at and share themselves with the audience. The result is usually an audience who feel they have been 'touched' by the performers and performers who feel that they are fantastic people. I have seen children's self-confidence and responsibility really grow through successful performance.

9   **Inhibited children** soon 'come out' within a safe, non-judgemental environment and with regular classes.

10   **How to use the chapters**. After reading this introduction, begin on Chapter 2, as it gives a basic grounding. You do not have to work through a whole chapter before you begin another — two or more chapters can run concurrently. (See Lesson Formats in Chapter 8.) Ideally, work on Chapter 3 should start a little after you begin Chapter 2. Material from the other chapters can be brought in at any time.

    It is important to start with Chapter 2 because it gives exercises on how to control a movement class; that is, how to start, move and stop with control and creativity. I do not suggest that you work through from page 1 to the end of the book, although this approach could work for some. Pick out exercises to suit you.

It is important, however, to *read* the whole chapter, even though you will not do every exercise in it. Comments, ideas for presenting the exercises, insights and complementary activities occur throughout the whole chapter and can be useful additions to the exercises you do want to do. Thus, if you want to give your children a taste of mask work by doing exercises 1, 2 and 3, read the whole of Chapter 5. The comments at the end of a series of exercises are most important, as are the introductions to the different chapters.

11 If the **materials** mentioned are not available, substitute with something you have at hand; for example, use a piece of string, coloured ropes or strips of material for a ribbon, or a saucepan and spoon for a drum. Most materials suggested are inexpensive or free. The children will enjoy their classes more if you have some exciting materials to work with and if you treat your materials with respect.

12 **Numbers and space** often help to determine a teacher's views of movement lessons. How many children and what space to use varies from school to school. How many children you can cope with at once depends on you and the children. There are no hard and fast rules or ways of coping with this. See point 3 in the introduction to Chapter 8 (page 103) for some ideas.

13 **Quotations marks** are used throughout the handbook to show when the teacher is speaking to the children. Sometimes part of an exercise is written in quotation marks; for example, 'Find a space and sit down in it.' Other parts of the exercise might be written in indirect speech; for example, The children find a space and sit in it.

14 **Standard games**, such as Tag or Grandmother's Footsteps, and games you make up yourself can be used in a movement class if you feel it relevant. I have not dealt with games here because there are plenty of other books available on that subject.

15 **Use ideas that the children give you**. Children often know their own needs very well, and there might be a deeper reason than you realise for them wanting to do something.

16 **The cassette recording** which accompanies this book has been designed to provide the music and sound components of the exercises.
Side 1 presents a selection of music for a variety of movements: walking, running, skipping, big and small shapes, rolling, crawling, jumping, balancing and turning. Also on Side 1 are sound effects and special music to accompany them: trains, wind, circus, water and fire.
Side 2 has fantasy music for certain activities suggested in the book: The Wizard, A Walk in the Forest, relaxation and warm-up exercises.

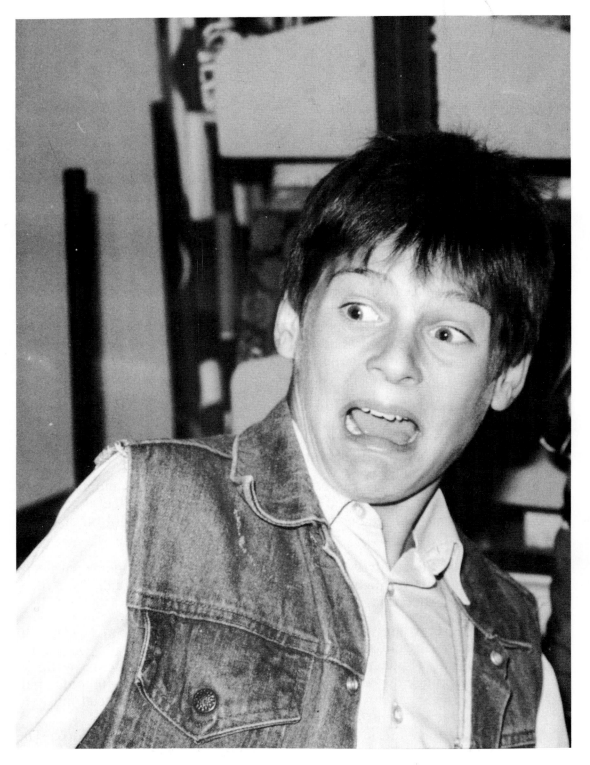

Don't be scared to try out your own ideas!

17 **Dance** is an outflow of energy, and clear, communicative movements are more effective than shuffly, small ones. A dancer explores and plays with energy. The audience can share and enjoy this energy if the dancer's movements and emotions are clear and purposeful.

18 **The glossary of special terms** which follows will help to clarify terms used with special meanings in this book.

Special Terms

Audience	A group of people with whom the performer shares his work.
Basic movements	Movements done as part of everyday life.
Carrying the mask	A term used in mask work to denote the change in a person's body when they put on a mask. In order for the mask performer to carry off the illusion that he has become a different person, he must allow the mask to change the rest of his body. If there is not enough change, or if the change is not in keeping with the mask, the mask cannot be said to be carried.
Cause	To act upon oneself or the environment, resulting in changes to oneself or the environment. 'Conscious cause' means to take responsibility for your actions at the same time.
Centre	To stand at centre or to be centred, standing straight and still, full of potential energy (see Chapter 2, Exercise 6, page 18).
Common space	The environment.
Create	To express one's inner self in a material or abstract form.
Energy	The creative force, which is physical (moves muscles), mental (creates mental pictures) or spiritual (awareness of beauty, love, etc.).
Fantasy	The creation of an environment other than the one which is agreed upon as reality, by the use of illusions and mental pictures.
Freeze	To suspend movement, not necessarily standing straight and centred, but holding whatever position one was in at the time of the order to freeze.
Get into mask	To open oneself to the mask in order to be changed physically and mentally and so be able to carry the mask.

Get out of mask
To let go of the feelings, viewpoints and physical characteristics created by opening oneself up to the mask, and become one's everyday self again.

Gypsona
The brand-name of plaster-impregnated bandages used for mending broken limbs — great for making masks.

Illusion
A mental picture which tends to become fixed and can be communicated to and shared by others.

Mental picture
A picture created in the mind which can have colour, shape, taste, density, smell, etc.

Stillness
A moment of stillness happens when a person who is moving freezes momentarily so that he/she or the audience can experience the position. This can be used either for effect in a performance, or to help the students become more aware of the shapes they are making as they move. Moments of stillness always give pieces greater visual effect and contrast.

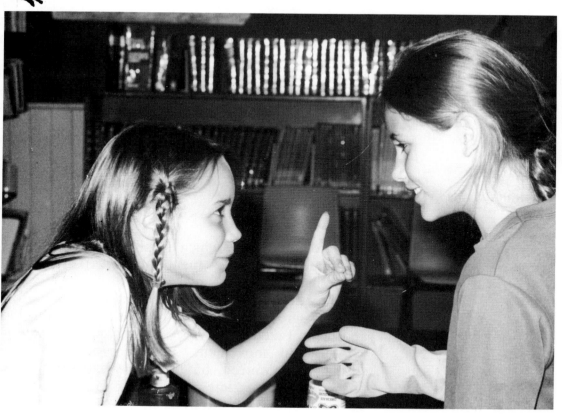

chapter 2:   the basic skills

Introduction

Principles of Creative Movement

Creative movement lessons should contain some or all of the following:
1   Use of space.
2   Use of energy.
3   Discovery of movement.
4   Discovery of time.

Use and Awareness of Space

To enable children, especially infants, to become more aware of their environ-ment and more confident within it, the teacher must devise creative exercises for them.

Use and Awareness of Energy

The teacher, through the use of creative situations, draws the children's atten-tion to the different ways and degrees of using physical energy. This is done through working in contrasts; for example, hard and soft, smooth and jerky, movement and stillness. These concepts are taught in conjunction with the dis-covery of basic movements.

Discovery of Movement

Through creative situations the children are made aware of basic movements and how they can use them to express themselves.

8

Lewis' Man Friday — illustration of a part he wished to have in his class play.

The movements are:

walking	balancing
running	turning
jumping (bouncing)	expanding
swaying	contracting
rolling	

These are combined with the different ways of using energy and explored within a given space during a certain amount of time.

Time

Slow or quick tempo — how long the piece takes, how long it takes to go from one point to another, for example, by a curved or straight pathway.

Other Factors in Creative Movement

Levels

Children should be encouraged to perform the movements low (near or on the ground), high (on toes or stretched towards the ceiling), medium (at normal or near normal walking level).

Relaxation and Stillness

The children should be encouraged to hold a shape that they have made and be silent whilst they do it (statues).

Relaxation. Children lie on the ground and are encouraged to relax and be completely still. (This fosters an awareness of stillness and an awareness of the body.)

Time, Space and Energy

Time, space and energy are the vehicles for exploring any kind of movement, from simple games to choreographed dances. They all take place in a given space at a certain speed or speeds (time) and require various amounts of energy.

I shall first deal with spatial work because it is by far the most complex of the three factors that influence movement. A child's awareness of himself as a unit in space — be it in a room, as a member of a school or a nation, or as a being on a planet or part of the cosmos — has direct influence on his self-image and his relationship with others.

Awareness of Space

This is a good way to start any kind of movement programme with any age group. I use this in kindergarten, with children in their first weeks of school and with adults who are beginning movement courses with me (I change the language accordingly, of course).

To explore space gives greater physical and mental self-control. In the series of exercises that follow we will look at two types of space: *personal space* and *common space*.

Personal space is the child's body and the space directly around it. It includes his mind and his vision of the world, which can be constructive or destructive.

Common space is the space shared by one child with others; for example, the room, the planet. There the child meets with others and has to communicate to them in order to survive. How he communicates varies according to the situation.

The exercises are given here in the order that I think is best. They can be broken down and spread over as many lessons as you like. It is up to the teacher to decide what best suits her children.

EXERCISE 1   Personal Space: Making a Room

Each child is given a piece of coloured rope of a length suitable to mark out a space on the floor for him to sit in. He is asked to find a space and do this. His rope must not touch anyone else's when it is on the floor and must meet at the ends. The shapes will, of course, vary (as in the diagram below).

Rope shapes will vary.

The teacher's dialogue might say something like this:

'This is going to be your special place — your room — make sure there is some space between your room and everyone else's . . .
'Sit in your room.
'Put your hands on the rope — that is the edge of your room. Run your hands around the rope — all the way round till you come back to where you started. Do the same with eyes closed, feel the rope all the way round . . . this is the edge of your room. Now open your eyes, sit and look at me.
'This is your room, you can make it anything you want. It doesn't have to

be like this room — it can be made of rainbows, feathers, a bubble, anything you like. It's your room. Put your hands on the floor. Close your eyes and see what the floor of your room is made of. Get a picture in your head — see the floor in that picture, the colour, what is it made of? Open your eyes and start to build the floor. (*Encourage the children to move.*)
'When you have finished your floor, sit on it . . . close your eyes and see the walls of your room. What colour are they? What are they made of? (*Children might want to whisper it to themselves.*) What's the door like? See the door in your picture and see the walls right up till you see the ceiling.'

The questions that you ask the children when they make up their mental pictures will vary according to age and ability. These are suggestions for you to adapt as you wish.

'Open your eyes, get up and build the walls of your room . . . put in the door . . . stand and put your hands on the door; keep them there so that I can see where the door is. And now the ceiling. Reach up and make the ceiling; make sure you know what it is made of and put it there. When you have finished, sit and look at me.
'Now you have made your room but you need to put some things in it, your things, things that you like, anything you want. Trees and rainbows, rocks and birds or trains and aeroplanes — you know because it's your room. Curl up, close your eyes and see the things that you want in your room. Now, keep your eyes closed, see your things in the places you want them. Where do they go in your room? Get a picture of them.
'Open your eyes and put your things in your room . . .
'When you have finished, sit and look at me. Now you have made your own room, it is different from anyone else's, it is special. Look around at it, look at the floor, the walls, the ceiling, the special things. Find out where you sleep and lie down, see what it feels like to lie in your room.'

If you want, you can end the first lesson here, or you can go on to Exercise 2. If you wish to end here, finish something like this:

> 'Sit up, look at your room and say aloud "thank you room". We are going to do something else now so we will put the rooms away till the next time. Pick up your rope and shake it in the air with a sound. Give me your ropes. Thank you.'

Comments

1 The above exercise has been written step by step, with working, to give you an idea of how I would do it with children. The exercises that follow will be less wordy, as I now leave it to the teacher to develop her own words.

2 I have used repetition in Exercise 1; for example, 'this is your room' is repeated several times in order to reinforce this concept. I use a soft voice to begin an action, then raise the volume a tone to encourage greater interest or movement.

3 Young children might need help or quietening down at times, that's fine, take the time to do it.

4 Do not worry if young children cannot use their imagination very well on request, it will come with practice. Their 'rooms' might be a little slapdash, but that's all right. They usually have fun and get a good idea of personal space from doing it.

5 Children should not talk much or break concentration during this exercise, but discussion, creative writing, painting, etc. can follow, with exciting results.

6 Children rarely bother about where they get the materials to build their room. If the question arises, when you tell them to build the floor or walls, etc., the materials can come out of the air or from outside the edge of the room. Normally I don't give any directions on this but I do not allow walking about the class during building time, in fact the children stay in their rooms during the entire exercise.

7 It helps if the children whisper things about the walls, floor, contents of the room to themselves during mental picture-making time.

8 Say thank you, usually verbally, to a tool that has helped you in movement classes. This creates respect for and awareness of props.

EXERCISE 2   Personal and Common Space: the Treasure Chest

Now the children make themselves secure in their personal spaces and then emerge to explore common space.

Make a class treasure box.

The children can collect things themselves or you can surprise them with 'treasures' you have assembled yourself. The treasures can be old jewellery, ribbons, bits of Christmas tree decorations, anything small enough to be held in a child's hand and fascinating to the 'owner'. A chocolate box or similar receptacle can be used for the chest, which can be of any size.

The rooms are re-made quickly if it's the beginning of a new lesson (see Comment 3 on page 12) and the children are called from their rooms in turn to the treasure box to find a treasure. They keep the treasure in cupped hands as they return to their rooms — it's their secret.

The children keep their treasures in their hands, stand, and when you say 'go' quietly go out of their rooms to find a partner. They stop opposite their partner, exchange a look at each other's treasures, then go to stand in front of someone else. This goes on a few times then bang the tambourine to signal that they all go back to their rooms. If you have no treasure chest, they can mime having a treasure.

EXERCISE 3   Exploring Common Space

The children now find hiding places for their treasures somewhere in their rooms. They stand up, ready to leave their rooms (this time the treasure stays). For this exercise I have developed a series of movements to encourage the children to inter-relate. You can evolve your own, of course.

a   'Go round the space, using any movement you like, and look at each room; see the shape of it. Make a pathway around the rooms (not inside).'

b   One child goes to visit someone else in their room. The host shows the visitor around, the visitor says 'thank you' and returns to his own room. (I usually let one half of the class visit the other half and then they swap.)

c   The children come out of rooms and stand in front of a partner, looking at the partner's face. They note hair colour, eye colour and shape of face. They shake hands with partners and say 'hello' (perhaps use name too). They pause, then go on to another partner to do the same thing.

d   Making a face. The children sit in their rooms and are asked to see if they can change their faces. They all make different faces, as many as they can.

'Find one you think is the best and hold it. Now go back to your everyday face. Now make your different face, the one you showed me a moment ago. Now back to your everyday face.
'Come out of your room, find a parner and stand in front of him. Have a look at each other's real face — see hair colour, eye colour, shape of mouth, nose, everything you can; pretend you've never seen that face before.
'Now change. Make the other face — pull your face into a different shape. Hold it, look at each other, laugh or whatever you need to do. Now, quick! Go back to normal. Let the laughter go and find another person. Be your everyday face again. Let the laughter go, you don't need it for the new person (and repeat).

e   Physical activities such as making big or small shapes with partners, hugs, pats on the head, clapping the other person's hands, etc.

Comments

1   *The lessons all end the same way*: as with Exercise 1 say 'Thank you, room', shake out the ropes and put them away.

2   You could make several lessons out of Exercise 3.

3   *At the beginning of every lesson* after the original room was made, the teacher should ask the children to put their ropes on the floor and sit inside them, then quickly talk them through reconstructing the walls, floor, ceiling and furniture. It need not be as thorough as the first time and could only take a minute; in fact it might be extra fun to do it at high speed. However, the image of the room needs to be recreated afresh every lesson.

4   *The common space activities*, in which the children inter-relate with each other, need special care, since they can become giggly. To help prevent this and encourage concentration:
   a   Talk the children through each step whilst they are taking part in the activity, as illustrated with making faces.

b Bang a tambourine or have some other established method of getting the children back to their rooms. They only leave their rooms when you say 'go', and although they may go from one partner to another without returning to their rooms, they do return between each activity; for example, between looking at other people's rooms and visiting other people's rooms, or between making shapes together and shaking hands.

c Insist that they don't giggle. (Laughing or whatever when they look at the funny faces is all right, as long as they stop and become ready to see someone new when they change partners.) Talking them through while they do it will help here too.

d Encourage each child's interest in the partner's face and body. This can be done by suggesting that they look at physical features — hair colour, etc. It is important that the children look without significance; that is that they don't see a person as ugly, bad, etc. Try to reinforce the fact that the purpose of this exercise is just to look.

5 The 'Treasures' are useful as a homing and grounding device. Each time the children return to their spaces between activities, they take out their treasures, which are waiting for their return, and enjoy them for the moment. Relating to others, especially when you are asked to look directly at them, and being looked at yourself can be a little frightening. To go back to their personal space and take their unique object in their hands enables the children to feel special and secure again, with a real or imagined treasure.

6 These exercises can be repeated and added to at various stages throughout the year, as children can get more and more out of them. The rooms can become islands, space craft, ships or whatever you want (but it is best to use the concept of a room first). Later activities could take the form of a game for private and common exploration (see Chapter 6, page 71*ff.*).

EXERCISE 4 Personal and Common Space Combined, without Ropes

This is a more subtle change from personal to common space and back again.

a Ask the children to recreate their room in the same way as before, but this time without ropes. They can define the edges by putting their hands around an imaginary rope or walking the boundaries on the floor.

b When the rooms are recreated the children stand in them with eyes closed. You inform them, in whatever way you like, that some magic has taken place (use an instrument if you like). Their rooms have become 'able to move around this bigger space'. Wherever they walk, their rooms will be around them.

c The children open their eyes and begin to walk. Ask them to put their hands out to where the walls of their rooms are, so that other people won't walk into their walls. The aim is to have all the children walking round the room, each aware of their own individual space, with their arms slightly away from their sides. They won't bump into each other if they are aware of the walls around themselves and others. Tell them: 'The walls are coming with you everywhere you go, the ceiling floats above your head, every step you take, the floor of your room comes with you, so you can walk on it. Walk slowly, smoothly and carefully.' Encourage the children to focus on their room as they move around. 'Let people glide past you as if they are ghosts, keep looking at the walls, the floor and the ceiling of your room, everything outside them is a bit hazy. Keep very much to yourself.' They could even close their eyes.

d   The children stop, still feeling their rooms about them. 'Now make your rooms disappear by waving your hands all around your body' (or any other way you wish — magic word, scarf, etc).

e   'Now the walls have gone. You can see wherever you look, clearly. Have a look at other people. Don't do anything, just look. Look at an object in the classroom that you like. Now go and stand by it, touch it.'

f   'Walk away from the object and freeze. Close your eyes, make the room around yourself, open your eyes.' Repeat Part c of this exercise.

g   The children flip from personal to common space, back to personal and into common again. There are many exercises to enable them to experience common space as in e above. I will list some more below, but of course it is best for you to choose or make up ones that suit your children.

i   'Find partners. One take the other round the room and show them some of the things you like. Tell your partner what it is you are showing them. Tell them about it and why you like it. Freeze, move away from your partner. Close your eyes and quickly make your room around yourself,' (as in c).

ii   'Find a partner, and have a look at them for a moment. Now look only at their hair; what colour is it? Is it curly, wavy or straight, long or short? Touch it. Freeze now. Forget your partner — they have nothing to do with you. Think of your own hair. Touch it. Do you know what colour it is?

Is it curly, wavy or straight? Long or short? . . . Freeze.

'Now open up and look at your partner again. Think only of your partner as if there were no-one else in the world. Look at your partner's arm. Notice if the skin is showing or if it is covered by clothes. Can you roll up the sleeve and see the skin underneath? Touch the skin. Are there any freckles, scratches or hairs? Can you see the shape of the bones? Freeze . . . now forget about your partner. Look at your own arm.'

And so on. Clothes, torso, legs, feet, hands, whatever you feel is appropriate, having the children flip from another person's body to their own each time. This doesn't have to be done all in one lesson.

EXERCISE 5   Sharing Personal and Common Space

By now the children should be able to create a room around themselves without 'building' it physically at all. They should be able to 'go in' on request (maybe with a magic word or sound) and then 'come out' and be aware of others. Use 'go in' and 'come out' if you like.

a   Children in pairs go into their rooms, standing next to but not in contact with their partners. Then they walk around the room (they can walk away from each other and go in different directions) totally oblivious of their partners.

On command: 'Come out and find your partner, hold hands and go round the room together, moving in the same way as each other, in any ways you both like. Freeze, let go of partner's hand, "go in", move along', and so on. Bang! (tambourine). 'Sit in space.'

After the exercise you could discuss the difference in feeling between the two types of relating, perhaps with some writing and drawing.

b   In pairs. Child **A** goes into his room while Child **B** watches him. **A** begins to walk around the room, unaware of but watched by **B**. On command, **A** comes out and joins **B** and they do a similar movement or mirror each other. Repeat, with **A** changing from being 'in' and unaware of B to coming out and joining **B**. Freeze, and end by sitting in a space.

EXERCISE 6   Standing at Centre

This exercise is designed to prepare children for the moments of stillness needed for starting and finishing basic movements, fantasy or mask work.

Tell the children to put their rooms around themselves and stand very still. Imagine they have a rope going from above their head, down through the centre of the body, through the middle of the legs, to the floor. You could demonstrate with a piece of rope. Rope and body is straight.

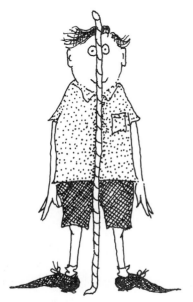

Standing at centre.

Head sits lightly on top of spine, shoulders relaxed (not soldier-like), arms relaxed, (shake them, let them fall). Legs and spine do the main work of holding up the body. This is known as 'standing at centre', because the line of balance is going through the centre of the body or, more simply, because there is an imaginary line running down the centre of the body. It is the same as 'stand in the room' and is used as a starting or quietening down position. It is passive, but ready for action, not slumped; at rest, but filled with latent energy.

Movement and Stillness

This is a bridging section between space work and any other creative movement you want to do. It gives you the basic formula for starting, moving and stopping children when working in a space, so that you are in control. Many teachers have trouble controlling movement classes and lack of control often means that the basics have been ignored. It can be used in conjunction with exploring personal and common space, as in Exercise 3 on page 13, or as part of an exploration of the basic movements.

EXERCISE 7   Starting, Moving and Sitting in a Space

a   Children move around the room and stop to various tambourine commands. They sit down without touching anyone (in a space). Spaces can be indicated on the floor by such things as pieces of tape, a rope (indicating 'the room', or even a chair to sit on. As you go round the room each child can say, 'I am . . . . . . this is my space'.

The following activity is not imperative, but can work well if each child stands up and makes a shape before saying the words.

'Stand up.'

(Shake tambourine.) 'This is running — run'

(Big bang on tambourine.) 'Run and sit on your piece of tape' (or whatever).

Reinforce the three commands:

Stand up.

Run (with sound from tambourine).

Go back to place and sit (on big bang from tambourine) or find another place.

b   Do the same exercise with walking (using a different tambourine sound) or other movements — hopping, skipping, creeping, etc.

c   Different levels and speeds can also be used; for example, walking tall or bent over, walking lightly or stamping, stamping whilst holding the body bent over.

d   Use different directions: forwards, sideways, backwards, etc.

Comments

1   A different, distinct sound needs to be made for each of the movements the child is asked to do. For example, hopping: a short tap on the tambourine with the finger, running: shake the tambourine, walking: bang the tambourine with the flat of your hand.

2   Let the children control each other. When they pick up the idea, one child can come out and go through the directions with the tambourine, instead of the teacher.

3   Commands and sounds must be very clear and direct.

4   Each exercise must begin by standing up and end by sitting in a space (stillness).

5   When children are proficient at sitting in spaces, tape, ropes or chairs are no longer needed. The children will just find a space anywhere at the end of each exercise.

EXERCISE 8   Statues and Freezing

As dance and drama is always punctuated by stillnesses, all movement lessons must contain experiences of stillness.

Statues

a   Explain to the children that they are going to move around the room in various ways and when you call out something (an object or a person) they are to make a statue of it. Say that you will come round and look at the statues to see which ones really look and feel like the thing that you said. For example, say:

b   'Find a space and sit in it.'
(When everyone has done that) 'Now stand.'
'Show me a tall walk.' (With tambourine sound.)
'Stop! Make a statue of someone eating an ice cream. Hold it very still. I am coming to look.'

c   'Move around now, making your body very small and creeping on your toes.' (Make appropriate sound.)
'Stop! Show me a statue of someone asleep.'

d   Carry on with alternate moving and statues until you wish to end. 'Find a space and sit in it.'

e   This can tie in with themes done in other lessons — animals, letters of the alphabet, parts of the body (make a statue pointing your finger, standing on one leg). Groups and number-work can also be brought in. 'Make a line, make a circle with your body,' or, instead of statues, groups could be used; for example. 'Make 'groups of four, make groups of three (etc.) and stand still. Now run round the room, stop! Get into groups of five. Lines, circles or group statues can be made by groups. 'Make a train with three people, make a mountain with five people and hold it as a statue.'

Comments

1   Enter into the fun of the moments of stillness with the children. Look at them when they are still and see what their bodies are saying. Sometimes, as I walk around, I bump into or trip over a child because he/she was so still. 'You were almost invisible!' The children really enjoy that. Otherwise they feel that stillness is a restriction rather than a pleasure.

2   You could encourage children to portray certain things by their statues. For example, the ice cream: 'I want to see if you really like the taste of your ice cream, if you are biting it or licking it. If it comes in a tub or a cone or on a stick. Taste the flavour of it, see it there in your hand, now hold it.'

3   Statues don't make sounds.

4   Allow one child to stand out and go round commenting on the statues, if you feel they can do so without being disruptive.

Freezing

Freezing has the same effect as statues: to create moments of stillness.

a Perhaps an explanation: 'An ice block is frozen. When it is put in the fridge to freeze it becomes very cold and very hard. You could bang it on the table and it would be as hard as a piece of wood, because it is frozen. We can make our bodies look like a frozen ice block if we hold them very still and stiff. Watch me. I am going to move my body, and when I say "freeze", I am going to stop in whatever position I happen to be in.' (Demonstrate.)

b 'See how when I said "freeze" I didn't stand up straight again — I held my body in exactly the same way as I had it when I said "freeze". My arms were out so I kept them out. One leg was off the ground, so I held it off the ground. I'll show you again, this time you (pick one child) say "freeze".'

c Practise saying the word with the children if necessary and reinforce that freezing is holding whatever position you happen to be in when the word is said. It does not mean stand up straight.

d The procedure for practising can go like this, after children have sat in a space ready for action: 'Stand.' Give a movement; for example, running in a certain way. 'Freeze. Hold it. I'm going to see how still you can be. 'Now run in a different way.'
'Freeze,' and so on.

e Adaptations and developments can be made from that.

Comments

1 Most comments on the statues exercise are also relevant here.

2 One child can give directions to the others, saying 'freeze', giving a move-ment, etc.

3 Fast movements interspersed with freezes are best and most fun; they also demand more self control than slow movements.

Awareness of Time

Any movement exercises that you can devise to enable your children to become aware of time in any of its aspects will enable them to have a greater awareness of this particular aspect of movement. Here are two that I find useful.

EXERCISE 9 Fast and Slow

a Pre-arrange a repeatable route to be taken by the children; for example, around the edges of the classroom, across the room diagonally, from the blackboard to the bookshelf.

b Ask one or all of the children to go along this route as quickly as they can.

c Then have them repeat the route as slowly as they can.(Some might not complete it before everyone gets bored.)

d Point out that, although the distance was the same, it took different amounts of time to complete it because the movements were different.

You can get a different view of things when working with others.

e   Various movements could now be tried over the same distance — rolling, hopping, sliding on the stomach, walking with a sway, walking normally, crawling.

f   If you like, use some method of timing, such as a stopwatch, an eggtimer or even counting or clapping.

g   A chart could be made.

Ways of Moving	Running	Walking on Tiptoe	Rolling
Times	3 secs (5 claps)	1 min (100 claps)	15 secs (25 claps)
Distance (always the same, — from blackboard to shelf)	10 metres	10 metres	10 metres

Deductions can be made from the chart, such as the fastest movement, slowest, etc.

EXERCISE 10   Pathways

a   Again pick a route but this time find different pathways to get from start to finish — curved, straight, zig-zag.

b   Use the same movement, but vary the path you use.

c   You could use ropes to create different paths between the two points.

d   Make a chart recording times.

EXERCISE 11   Chronological Time

You can also look at chronological time's effect on movement, and have some fun.

a   Children show you how they walk now, naturally.

b   Go back in time — the children show how they walked when toddlers. What movements could they not do then that they can do now?

c   'How did you get around before you could walk? Show me.'

d   'Can newborn babies get around at all? Show me what a newborn baby looks like.'

e   Then take them up the scale again through (c), (b) and (a) again and then into the future:

f   'How will you walk when you're a teenager? an adult?' (Do they think they'll run as much then as they do now?) 'What happens to people's bodies when they get old? Show how you think an old person might walk. Can old people run the same as young people?'

g   Perhaps you can take it right to death, thus completing the circle; that is, a newborn baby has no movement around the space; a corpse has none. It will enable the child to get a clear perspective of himself in time and the cyclic patterns of life.

Pathways between two points: curved, straight and zig zag.

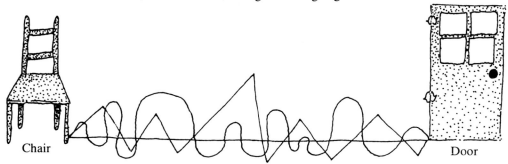

Chair   Door

PATHWAYS BETWEEN TWO POINTS: curved, straight and zig zag

Awareness of Energy

EXERCISE 12   Experiencing Energy

a   'Lie on the floor, relax.'
b   'Lift your arm into the air and hold it up.'
c   'Put it down again and sit up'
d   'What enables us to move that arm? Muscles, yes; bones too, but what moves the muscles? Energy. You can't see it but it's like breath or sunshine, electricity or heat from a fire. You can't see it but it's there.'
e   'Lie on the floor again.'
f   'Think about your right arm. Keep the arm still and, with your mind, just feel your arm lying there on the floor.'
g   'Fill your arm with energy and lift it up.'
h   'Hold it up, keep the energy in it.'
i   'Now let the energy drain out. What happens when the energy drains out?' (Does the arm fall?)
j   You can develop this exercise further. For example, when the arm is filling with energy, before raising it from the floor let it become fuller and fuller of energy. It might feel tingly or pulsate, but still don't move it. Finally, after a minute of feeling the energy in the arm, let the arm move. This can be linked to effort; for example, using more energy than needed to do a job. Mention the fact that people do give off energy vibrations from their bodies all the time.

EXERCISE 13   Outflowing Energy

As mentioned in the introduction, dance is an outflow of energy. Small, introverted movements are not nearly so effective as movements which send energy out.

a   'Extend your arm. Feel the energy go along the arm, leave the hand and hit the wall, like a beam.'

b   Do it with other parts of the body (See 'The Wizard', page 75, which gives this exercise in detail.)

Outflowing energy.

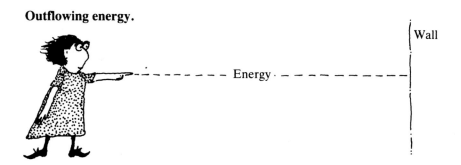

Energy

Wall

Comments

1   It doesn't matter whether you tell your children to let their energy leave their bodies as a beam from the fingers, face, chest or legs, to hit a point on the wall. (You can use other body parts, too, such as knee caps, elbows, backs.) The main thing is for the children to realise that movement, just like speech, emotion, painting or sport, uses energy, and that it is best if that energy flows in big, creative movements rather than small, tense ones.

2   Try dancing and keeping the energy trapped inside the body. It will be tense, jerky and inhibited — not very pleasant — but useful in some dance or drama situations. Trying the opposite will give you a better idea of energy outflow.

3   The more movement work you do with the children, the more you will become aware of their energy outflow.

EXERCISE 14   Hard and Soft Energy

a   Explore different actions and movements with both 'hard' and 'soft' energy: For hard energy: 'Imagine the air around you has become tangible — hard and solid. You can feel it when you put out your hand. To move through the space you have to push hard.' (Encourage pushing, chopping, kicking and wringing movements. A lot of energy must be used when moving with hard energy.)

For soft energy: 'Instead of opposing you, the air is helping you to move through the space.' (There is a light, soft feeling when you move with soft energy. Use waving, swaying, floating or rippling movements. Less energy needs to be used for soft energy movements.)

b   If you can find actions that make sounds, all the better. Try clapping hands with yourself or someone else. Different kinds of energy give different sounds — tongue clicking, jumping, pushing a chair or waving a piece of cloth, all with hard or soft energy.

Awareness of the Environment

Now that the children have become aware of personal and common space and can control their bodies within those forms of space, they need to look at what creates the space: the boundaries.

The space changes as the child moves from one environment to another. The environment controls the movements of a child; for example, the range of movement possible in a classroom is smaller than in a large park. A child needs to know his limits as this gives freedom to explore. I hope that the exercises below will suggest other boundary activities for you to try.

EXERCISE 15   Awareness of Boundaries

a   'What makes our classroom separate from the one next door? A wall. What else do walls do for us?' (Shelter from outside; tell us how much space we have; etc.) 'A wall can be as important to us as a human friend.'

b   'How is the floor like a friend?' (It holds us off the ground; we can sit on it; etc.)

c   'How is the ceiling like a friend?' (It keeps rain and sun off; something that the lights hang from; etc.)

d   'If you were walking down the street and someone that you know was coming towards you, what would you say when you met? You'd say "hello". Hello is a greeting for friends and other people we might meet. Sometimes objects can be as much part of your lives as people, like this room we come to every day.'

e   'Go and find your own spot next to a piece of wall, turn round, look at the wall.'
'Touch the wall with different parts of your body. Say "Hello wall".'
'Do the same with a different part of the wall.' (Repeat as many times as appropriate.)
The floor is dealt with in a similar way. (It is best to encourage whispering when "hello" is said.)
The children reach as high as possible, look up and whisper 'Hello ceiling'. With older children a more sophisticated exercise might be needed or you

might just have some fun doing the exercise as it is written here or putting on different types of voices.

EXERCISE 16   Awareness of Objects within the Space

a   Each child is asked to look around the space and locate an object that he really likes, then to go and stand by it.

When all the children are beside their objects, a series of commands encourages them to be aware of the object in relationship to themselves in different parts of the room. For example, 'Go as far away from the object as you can while still being able to see it. Go somewhere in the room where you can't see your object. How far away from your object can you be and still be able to touch it? How near to it can you get without touching it? Look at it from different positions in the room. Does it look the same from different positions?'

Abby (kindergarten). **Awareness of people, their bodies and their movements is increased by creative movement work.**

chapter 3:   the basic movements

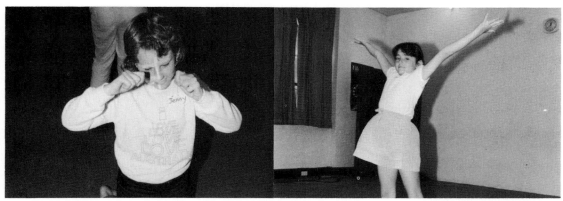

A big shape.

Introduction

This basic movement section should only be attempted when the children you are teaching can start, carry out, and stop an action on command and sit in a space and work without touching others. Of course, some of the basic movements can be done as part of the exploration of common space, as in Exercise 3 (page 13) or Exercises 7 and 8 (pages 18 and 19). However a complete exploration of the basic movements comes with physical control. If the children often get out of control when working on this chapter, take them back to movement and stillness work and look at self control in that simple way again. Reinforce it more strongly during such a refresher lesson.

In the basic movement section the teacher encourages the children to consciously explore everyday movements, exaggerate and stylise them and then string them together to make a dance.

Each movement is to be as distinct as possible and visually pleasing. For example, in everyday life we often go for economy of effort — a flick of the wrist might shut the door instead of a turn and full extension of the arm. In creative movement, small shapes are made as tiny as possible, with the energy drawn in; big shapes stretch as far as they possibly can; walking and running are done as you would never see them on the street.

So, although the children already know most of these movements subconsciously and use them in various forms many times a day, the teacher makes them conscious actions, gives them each a name and encourages their exploration, using time space and energy in a variety of ways.

During a movement, energy flows through the body and out into the environment (see 'The Wizard', page 75). Thus an arm is raised till it reaches the required height; it is clearly held there until the energy that took it there leaves via the fingertips. (It might be held for only an instant, as with a flicking motion, or for several seconds, as with a big extension.) A kick with the foot is so clear that energy leaves the toes; a curled body is not at rest but radiates energy whilst the curling motion is held. This is the reason why moments of stillness during the dance (freezes and statues) are of such great importance.

For the purposes of this handbook, we shall take some of the basic movements and show how children can explore them. These movements are:

1 Walking, running, rolling, crawling (travelling movements).

2 Jumping (bouncing), big shape, small shape (expansion and contraction).

3 Balancing, swaying and turning (known as 'the other movements').

There are, of course, others which you can explore. I hope that by tackling the movements I have given, you will be inspired to try other movements and branch out to create your own exercises.

Definitions

Travelling movements enable the child to move around the space.

The other movements colour the travelling steps. They are done in a smaller space than the travelling steps and stillness usually grows out of them. Thus a dance might look like this:

A Dance.

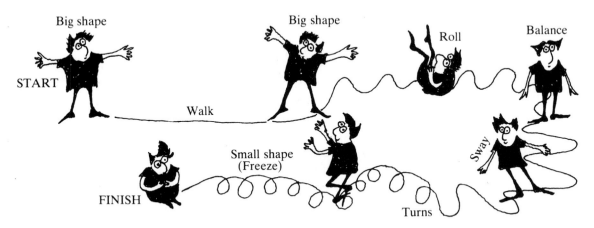

Of course, the difference between travelling movements and other movements is not clear cut: running can be done on the spot whilst a series of big shapes could move you quite a way round the room. But for the purposes of this book I will keep the definitions. You can of course experiment with using other movements as travelling movements and vice versa, but this is best done after a certain amount of progress with the basic movements has been made.

Moments of stillness are used mainly with the movements other than travelling movements. A stillness is right when a shape feels good to stay in for a few moments, especially big shapes, small shapes and balances. Stillness stops the busyness of the dance. A dance gets too busy to watch if it is all movement. A moment of stillness allows energy to leave the body and enables the dancer to collect himself for the next series of movements.

Levels can be explored — high, low and medium.

Speeds can be varied within a dance. A dance done all at the same speed becomes difficult to watch.

Accompaniment can be:

1   Percussion, which has the advantage of allowing the child to play an instrument as well as dance. It's simple rhythmically as well as instrumentally.

2   A tape or record, which can be used in two ways: for rhythm, as in 'Bouncing' (see page 32) or for atmosphere, as in chapter 6. This exposes children to various types of more complex music.

3   The child's own voice, which is great for sound exploration and development and helps the child understand the quality of the movement he is performing.

4   The teacher's voice. By that I mean the teacher telling a story or giving directions whilst the children move. The voice, when varied in tone and pitch to suit the mood of the movements, can be most effective. (see chapter 6).

Comments

1   The teacher does not need to stick to one type of accompaniment whilst exploring the various basic movements. It's best to expose the children to all types at one time or another; for example, for running, start with a tambourine accompaniment and later ask children to create their own sound with voices or sounds instead of, or as well as, the tambourine. Later you could make a story about someone losing their dog and having to run to one spot accompanied by some frantic orchestral music, freeze, look for the dog then run on again to another spot, freeze, listen for the dog, run on again, and so on. Of course, these can be done in the same lesson or they can be combined with other things and part of several lessons.

2   I have given accompaniment directions in the following pages; use them or create your own as you wish.

The Movements: General Exploration

Walking

'This is a walking sound.' (Regular bangs on the tambourine, using the flat of the hand.) 'Each time you hear a beat take a step.' (Get through this quickly in Year 3 and above). Intersperse with freezing and sitting in a space.

Now make up a simple story to explore walking; perhaps a journey over different surfaces and different landscapes, including mud, water, hill (up and down), long grass, heavy loads. Tell the story while the children vary their walking speeds, levels, etc. accordingly. Use taped music and make voice sounds where appropriate.

Running

This is dealt with in a similar way to walking. The tambourine sound is a brisk shake. Use the lost dog for a story idea.

Rolling

1   Percussion sound is scratching the cloth of the tambourine with the finger nails.

2   Encourage children to find as many shapes as possible to make when rolling: straight out, curled, summersaults. Try freezing and making big stretched shapes, as below.

A big stretched shape.

3   Allow children time for experimenting and pick examples from what comes up in their work. 'Can you roll with one leg in the air like . . .?' Find voice sounds too.

Crawling

1   Tambourine: regular light, sharp flicks with the finger, at the same rhythm to which the hands are put down on the floor when crawling.

2 Crawling in different directions, face up or down. What body parts are used for support?

3 You could use an animal story for a crawling story to act out.

Jumping

1 Percussion: a big bang on the cymbals.

2 There are a great variety of jumps, so encourage the less common ones; for example, scissors, bunny hops, turn, legs crossed, hand springs (big bunny hops!).

3 Jumps are best done with a travelling movement. You could talk the children through small sequences, using different travelling movements and encouraging different jumps. For example:
   a Run, jump, freeze.
   b Walk, jump, freeze.
   c Roll, jump, freeze.
   d Crawl, jump, freeze.

4 Percussion for the above would be in the same order:
   a Shake the tambourine, bang the cymbals and say 'freeze'.
   b Beat the tambourine, bang the cymbals and say 'freeze'.
   c Scratch the tambourine, bang the cymbals and say 'freeze'.
   d Flick the tambourine, bang the cymbals and say 'freeze'.

Bouncing

1 This is slightly different to jumping. You can bounce various parts of the body; for example your hand, your head, the top half of your body, one leg.

2 Percussion: rhythmic taps with a stick on the cymbals or beaty disco music, which is especially good for this one.

3 Other movements like walking, making shapes or swaying, can be done with a bounce. A little disco sequence can be made of: walk, big shape, small shape, sway, all done with bounces and appropriate hand movements. Children of all ages think it's great to dance like 'Countdown'.

Big and Small Shapes

Except with five year olds, I usually teach these two movements at the same time.
1 The percussion sound varies with the speed required for the movement (see below): either a light sharp bang on the cymbals or several slow scrapes of the cymbals together.

2　'Make a big shape, not just a big X, but something more interesting. When you hear the crash of the cymbals, fall down quickly into an interesting small shape.'
'Crash!' (They fall down. Inspect shapes and comment on any unusual ones.)

3　'In a moment you will hear a different sound. When I rub the cymbals together, I want you to grow very slowly, bit by bit, up into another big shape — a different one from the one before.' (Give directions, examples and comments where necessary.)

4　The two percussion sounds denote speed and can be used with either shape.
'Sink down.' (Scrush, scrush, scrush sound from the cymbals.)
'Shoot up into a big shape.' (Ting! on the cymbals.)
'Now fall down into a small shape.' (Ting! on the cymbals.)
'Grow slowly up into a big shape.' (Scrush, scrush, scrush.)

5　When the children catch on to the sound directions you can perhaps omit the verbal ones. 'I am not going to tell you big or small, if you are small then the next movement will be big, if you are big the next movement will be small. Take your speed from the cymbals.'

6　If the children have too much difficulty with this, don't do it. Watch for variety and originality of shape and compliance with your sound instructions on speed.

7　Monsters or Creatures are a good creative idea. Start with a small shape, rise into a big monster shape, sink down again, rise as another monster/creature, and so on.

Balancing

1 Experiment first with balancing on one part of the body. What single body parts can be balanced on? Then two body parts, then three, and so on, up to five.

2 An improvised dance can be made by flowing from one balance to another. The number of body parts in contact with the floor from one balance to another is now random; for example, two parts, followed by five parts, followed by three parts.

3 Percussion: each balance could be denoted by a shake of bells or castanets.

4 Taped music: I use Paul Horne and Yassar Latif's Music in the Taj Mahal for Flute and Voice' to create a floaty atmosphere while the children improvise their balancing sequences.

Swaying

1 Start on the floor, very relaxed. (You could do a relaxation exercise beforehand.)

2 'Gently sway one hand along the floor, feel the floor, now let it rest.'

3 This procedure is followed in the same way by the other hand, one leg, other leg, head. Sit up, sway top of body, stand, sway whole body on spot, then move round the room swaying.

4 Percussion: a rhymic sound to match the sway, on bells or castanets.

5 An improvisation called 'The Sea' could be done with scarves. Swaying as waves, big breakers, foam at the water's edge, sea weed, a jelly fish, etc.

Turning

Practise three types of turn, a small turn, a big turn and a half turn.
1 Small turn: go up on the toes and revolve on the spot.

2 Big turn: walk or run in a small circle. (I use a hoop for this with infants. They make a small turn inside the hoop, right in the middle, on their toes and a big turn by running round the outside of the hoop.)

3 Half turn: stand still and twist the torso.

4 Sometimes I ask the children to do one turn only; that is, to come back to the spot at which they started. You can make that easier by locating a spot on the wall in front of them before they start and then locating the same spot after completing the turn.

5 Turns can be made on different parts of the body, including knees, bottom, one foot or even hands.

6 A useful creative exercise is to imagine that the children each have a watering can full of water and are watering different-sized circular flower beds. Some have to step into the middle and do a small or half turn to water it. This gives the effect of pouring out energy as you turn, and will enrich the movements.

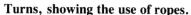

Turns, showing the use of ropes.

There are, of course, other basic movements with which you can experiment now that you have some ideas from the previous pages. You or the children can now make up new ways of trying the movements and different stories to encourage movement.

However, I've found that the above movements are enough to enable children to know what a movement is called and how to perform it. When this movement vocabulary is established, the children can begin performing dances. Even if only three movements have been explored, they can be linked to form a small dance.

Floor pattern for a series of turns:
use travelling steps between turns and freeze from time to time.

START   Run   Small turn   Skip   Big turn (Freeze)

FINISH   Jumps

Jump and turn   (Freeze)   Turn, kneeling   Roll

Dance Making

A dance is a series of movements linked together to form a sequence.

Ingredients. For the purposes of this handbook a dance is made up of travelling steps, such as running, walking, skipping or rolling, and more stationary movements such as balancing, swaying, expanding and contracting and moments of stillness (statues or freezing).

Motivation. A dance can be made to:

1 Tell a story. The movements and travelling steps are chosen because they are the most suitable with which to communicate the characters and events. The freezes highlight the other movements (see the comment on page 98).

2 To explore a particular mood or feeling such as emotions, the seasons or animals. The dance's movements, travelling steps and freezes will all be geared to exploring and suggesting the right mood or animal or human type.

3 To enjoy the basic movements, their contrasts and variety. This type of work has no theme as such. The accent is on the basic movements for their own sake.

4 There are other motivations — music, a picture or something else could be the main influence on the dance. Whatever the motivation, the basic movements chosen need to relate specifically to the motivation in mood, form, energy type and use of space. (Examples given in many parts of chapter 6.)

Always begin each dance from centre (or a specific starting position) and end with a freeze. If you used a theme on animals for example, the starting positions would be a stillness in the shape of the animal the dancer had chosen to portray, instead of at centre.

STAGE 1

(This can be used from Kindergarten to Year 6.) Give a task of three basic movements and freeze: for example, run, jump, big shape, freeze.
a   This activity is done singly or in pairs, with each child or pair in an allotted space. The space limits must be exact and children must adhere to them. (They can walk their group's special boundaries before beginning work.) After allocation of space the children work by themselves on the movements given for five or ten minutes, then each group shows the rest of the class.
b   With younger children I get the whole class to do this together first, and I use a percussion sound for each movement. The children use the whole space together. I then single out a few children at a time who do the sequence for the others, using the whole of the room or part of it. Gradually, after doing it all together, the little ones get the idea of what is needed and can practise a movement task alone or in pairs.

STAGE 2

As for stage 1, but with the addition of the children or yourself making up a story to go with the movements. For example:
Run: a pirate going up the boarding plank of an enemy ship;
Jump: the pirate jumps down onto the deck;
Big shape: the pirate lifts his cutlass, ready for action;
Freeze: he looks around, ready to fight.

STAGE 3

This should not be tried until children are ready; that is, until they have been through stages 1 and 2 (perhaps several times), and are conversant with the basic movements.

Now the children can choose a theme themselves. See what movements suit that theme and make a sequence from them. It is best to use the formula — starting position, three basic movements, freeze — to begin with. If the children want to use the theme of arguing and falling out with a friend, for example, they can explore that idea in whatever way they like, perhaps by trying out different movements or talking about them, or by play-acting the incidents, until they come up with some movements that would be best to show their theme. (Ask them to give you the names of the movements if possible.) They might say, 'Jump, run, big shape.' By using a start and a finish, the three movements, facial and body expression, speed, mood, floor pattern, sounds and whatever else they can, the children then make up their own dance.

STAGE 4

Children select their own themes and movements. Sequences can now be lengthened to more than three basic movements and children can be encouraged to use movement to express an idea or feeling which they want to communicate.

At this stage it is most important to get across to older children the point that they can use this as another form of communication and can point out things about which they have strong feelings and evoke emotions in others. Freezing can be anywhere in the dance, not only at the end, but wherever feels right (see 3 on previous page).

Props, music and stimuli such as hoops, ropes and scarves can also be used at this stage. (See chapters 4 and 6 for further dance making ideas).

Points to Note

Hands

Hands and arms are often forgotten, but can be a very expressive part of the body. Children should use their hands as a complement to the rest of their bodies whenever possible. Here are some ways to encourage hand and arm movement.

Concentrate on the Hands.

1 'How many shapes can you make with your hands?'

2 'Do any of them say something?' (For example, witches' hands, hands asking for something, happy hands, hands that look like a mountain, a bird, a ship.)

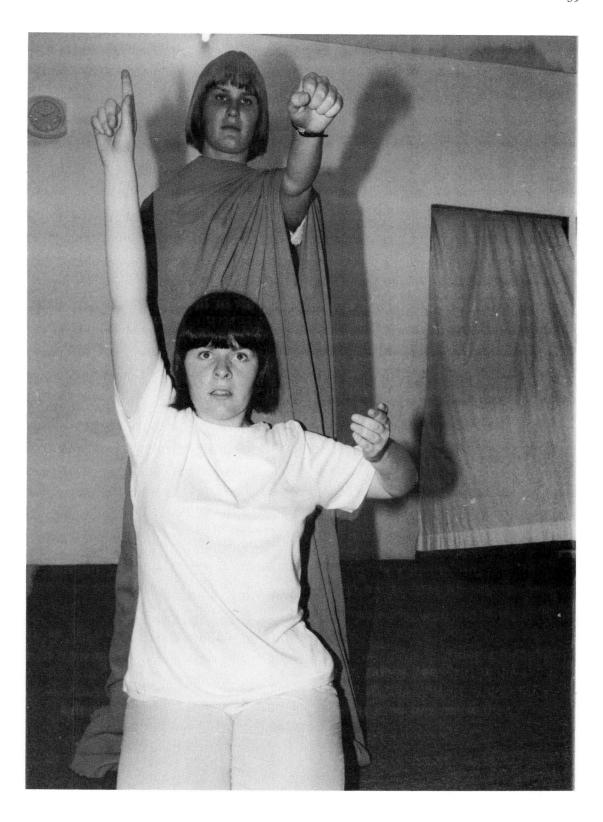

3 'Can you make a sound with your voice to go with the movement of your hands?'

4 'What sounds can your hands themselves make?' (Clapping in different ways, clicking, flicking.)

5 'What can the hands do to different types of music — hand dances, using fingers, part of hand, whole of hand, arms?'

6 'Start to move the rest of your body and let your arms lead you round the room. Let your body follow your arms both in direction and type of movement. Move with soft movements in curves.
'Move with hand movements in straight lines.
'How else can you move (with arms always leading)?
'Let your arms go to different parts of your body so that you have to go low, high, sideways or backwards.'

7 'Find a partner and let your hands have a conversation. Don't use your voice in any way.'

Bring the Hands into the Basic Movements

1 'Try running and using your hands in different ways. Are some ways better than others?'

2 'Now try other movements. How is it best to have your hands when balancing, or when in a small shape? Can you extend or contract the arms for a different effect? Can you make the shape exciting by the way you use your arms?'

3 'Try a movement using hard energy then soft energy. Does using a different type of energy (see Exercise 14, page 25) affect the movements that you make with your arms?'

4 Use different stimuli such as scarves, ribbons and light sticks, to encourage the use of arms.

5 Use different types of music — disco, flowing, marching.

6 Use different fantasies and dramas which accent the use of the arms, such as an octopus, trees, insectiverous plants, exploding stars.

7 Ask the children for ideas.

Rhythm

Rhythm is often there in the stimuli you provide, for example:
1 Percussion: The children quickly pick up the simple rhythm of one instrument giving a constant beat.

2 Taped music is more difficult. It often consists of many instruments and

sometimes many beats. I often use taped music as background to set the atmosphere and do not worry about dancing to it as such (although disco or rock often has a constant usable beat). When I use taped music with a constant beat, I get the children to clap or stamp it first, then I can see if they're catching on. With older children (year 2 upwards) I might get them to count a specific piece they are working on, especially if it's for performance. We might put sounds or words to the piece to help count the rhythm; for example for a tribal dance, 'Hugga Bugga, Hugga Bugga' gave us the one and two rhythm that the children needed to keep in step. A leader stood out in front to set the pace. I give very little rhythm tuition and let an awareness of rhythm evolve naturally. Just make it as easy as possible for the children by letting them clap, sing or whatever when rhythm is needed. Most children cannot cope with silent counting throughout a piece, so I do not enforce it.

3   Your own voice can be a rhythm guide for the children. For example,

'And they ran, ran, ran to all corners of the earth,
And when they had found their place *slowly* lay *down* and
slept and slept.'

Line one is much quicker, with a running rhythm, then in line two the words are drawn out and repeated, to slow the movement down.

4   Use rhythm for fun. When children have gained some confidence and freedom with movement I might give a lesson where I give a 'counting dance'. Movements are chosen for their formal feeling, the top of the body is kept straight, and arms are moved only to complement body shapes. Such movements might be — walk, stretch up on toes, turn. The sequence is then done to different counts in a very controlled manner; for example, to the count of four; 'Walk, two, three, four, stretch up on toes, two, three, four, turn, two, three, four, freeze, two, three, four.' I count out loud all the time until the children can do it. Then we might try counting two beats, three beats or syncopating like this:

'Walk and one and two and three (more a skip)
and stretch and one and two and three
and turn and one and two and three
and freeze and one and two and three.'

The children can find what movements suit what rhythms best. Some are best syncopated whilst others suit a slow rhythm. Then they can find out what rhythms suit different stories, emotions or themes.

Warm ups

Last, but definitely not least!
In fact, a warm up should be given at the beginning of every lesson, for at least three to fifteen minutes, depending on the length of the lesson and the needs of the children.
This section of the lesson is often done successfully to disco or other popular music and the children can bring in their own tapes.

Method 1   Using the Basic Movements

An excellent addition to a lesson when the children are learning the basic movements. I tell the children some movements and they memorise the names of them over a few warm ups. Then we do them in a set order to music at the beginning of every lesson for a few weeks. We do this as soon as the children have come into the room and found a work space each. It might go like this:
'Walk on the spot (using arms), freeze.
'Walk in different directions, freeze.
'Run on the spot, freeze.

'Run in different directions, freeze.
'Six rolls, freeze.
'Six jumps (all different), freeze.
'Expand, contract, freeze.
'Six balances (all different), freeze.
'Stand at centre.'
The children do this to different music every time, so it becomes a different dance.

Method 2   Isolation of Body Parts

Isolate each part of the body and move it independently of the rest. The body part can be bounced, swung, swayed or expanded and contracted. It is best to start at the head and work down to the feet.

Jonathon (Year 2). **If a story is experienced through movement it becomes very vivid for the child.**

This student played a tribesman who was at the bottom of the mountain.

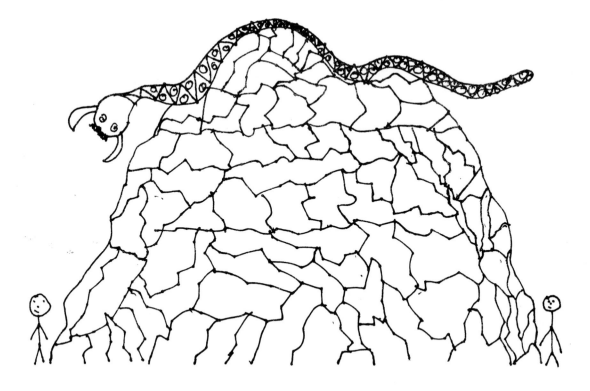

Method 3 Free movement

This is the part of the lesson where the children can take control. Just put on some music and go.

Especially with methods 1 and 2, one child can come out and direct the others by calling out each movement as necessary. (For Method 2: 'Bounce your heads up and down … Thank you' ('Thank You' stops the children bouncing their heads after a suitable time.) 'Bounce your shoulders … Thank you … Bounce your chest' etc. This enables children to take command of each other in a positive way which they really enjoy.

This diagram by James (*Year 6*) **shows some of the break and rap movements he has learned. He spends his time in my lessons choreographing, practising and teaching sequences to classmates. These are later performed to the rest of the school.**
Next term he will teach children from other classes too. All this has, of course, boosted James' self-confidence greatly.

The advent of rap and break dancing has changed the opinion of many adolescents — especially males — towards dancing. Not being a rap dancer myself, I let the more competent children teach the others the rap steps they know and we include them in our creative movement dances. Having tried shoulder spins on the floor in a Year 5 class, I'd say I prefer peer group teaching, or a professional could come in and teach the children a few things!

chapter 4: using objects to stimulate movement

Scarves

Scarves can be a physical manifestation of body energy — the arm moves and makes the scarf sway and the degree of energy used by the arm has different effects on the scarf. Hard energy (see Exercise 14, page 25) in the body makes the scarf flap rapidly and noisily. Soft energy makes the scarf glide slowly.

Light chiffon scarves are best, in bright colours.

What to Do With Scarves

How many different movements can be done with the scarf? Perhaps the children can explore by themselves or they might need questions to help them.

1 'Where can you hold the scarf?'
   (In the hands, teeth, between knees, under arm, etc.)

2 'How can you move it when you hold it in these different places?'

3 'What movements can you make using hard energy?'

4 'What movements can you make using soft energy?'

5 'Throw the scarf in the air and catch it.'

6 'Let it land on the floor and see what shape it makes. This could develop into fantasy work, the child could try to make the shape of the scarf on the floor with his own body.

7 'Use the scarf on your or someone else's body with hard and soft energy.'

8 'Twine the scarf around your body from the head, round and round the different parts of your body till you come to your feet. Do it to someone else.'

Make a Dance

1 'Find three favourite movements with the scarf.'

2 'Do them one after the other.'

3 'Find ways to exaggerate and make your movements bigger and clearer.'

4 Use voice, percussion and/or taped music to accompany it.

5 'Show it to the others, in starting position to begin with, freeze at the end.'

Make a Mask

Masks can be made from scarves. Put the scarf over the face as a veil, bandit style or any other way the children can find. (See further ideas, page 68.) 'Who are you? How do you move? What body part leads when you move?'

'Find a partner, make up a story about your characters and make a dance from the story.'

Mirroring

One child follows the path that the other makes with his/her scarf. Pictures and shapes in the air are made at different levels, with one child as the leader, then the other. They can stay in one spot or move around the room. Maintain eye contact between partners if possible. A dance can be made and practised in the same way as for 'Make a Dance' above.

Ribbons

Ribbons and scarves can be used in a similar way. The exercises given under the two headings are interchangable. Lack of materials need not limit your ideas.

Activities Using Slow and Fast

1 'Run round the room and make your ribbon fly out behind you. Can you watch your ribbon and run at the same time? Find a voice sound to make as you run.'

2 'Walk slowly round the room, dragging your ribbon. Make sure it touches the floor (take it for a walk). Watch your ribbon, see what different kinds of pathways it makes on the floor. Find a sound to go with this activity.'

3 'Make circles in the air — fast small circles, then slow big circles.'

4 'With a partner. One person standing on the spot moves the ribbon, making

patterns in the air. The other becomes the ribbon, moving as much of his body as he can in the same way as the ribbon is moving, using speed, direction, mood, etc.'

5   Make a dance using three favourite movements.

6   Mask work. The ribbon is worn on the body in some way to denote the character the child has chosen. For example, tied round the neck as a tie denotes a business man; tucked into the belt at back it becomes a tail; tied round the leg it indicates an invalid; tied on diagonally from shoulder to hip it means a champion. See what the children come up with, then carry on in the same way as directed in the Scarves Section.

Ropes

Coloured ropes are stronger than scarves or ribbons and can be used for more boisterous activities, such as tension — pulling and relaxing — and exploration of distances and levels, as shown below.

Free Exploration with Ropes

This can, in my experience, be very exciting. Ropes have certain connotations to children and the worst fears of the teacher are often realised with surprisingly positive effects, especially with slow learners. I have had children tie each other up, tie me up and tie themselves to chairs, and do other things which might have been though non-productive, such as play 'horses' with the ropes. However, I stayed on the side and watched and noticed that these activities were developing the children's sense of control and role play. They were constantly using language and, in a very free and easy way, they controlled and directed each other towards a goal and were pleased at achieving it. The children found amazing ways of moving when tied up and became most creative.

Direction

1   'With a partner, see how tight you can pull the rope (elastic is also good for this), now slacken it. Do you have to change position to do this?'

2   'Move round the room, keeping the rope taut. Do you have to have different ways of manoeuvring round people when the rope is taut than when it is slack?'

3   'With a partner, have one at each end of the rope and put the end of the rope round your waist. Turn round and round till you meet your partner in the middle. Make a shape together when you meet.'

4   'Make a picture on the floor with your rope and walk round the picture keeping your feet on the rope. Visit someone else's and do the same.'

5   Create shapes or pathways and make up fantasy pieces.

Simple shapes must be strong and clear to be most effective. Material can be worn to enhance body shapes.

Dance Making

1 'What shapes can you make with a partner, holding the ends of the rope?' If the rope (or perhaps a stick) is strong enough, counter-balancing in which the two children lean and sway, each trusting the weight of the other, can be tried. Or perhaps the children can try their movements while partially wound up in the rope. Winding or picking up the rope could be part of the dance.

2 a 'Make a pattern on the floor with your rope. Use three or four basic movements and create a dance in which your feet follow and stay on the rope.'
   b Allow free expression to music or sound, using the rope pattern on the floor or in the air to control the movements.

3 'The rope has become anything you like. Create a dance to show what it has become.' It could be a magic road to the stars (laid out on the ground); a ball gown (wrapped around the body); or a dog's lead (loosely round the neck). 'With a partner, make up a dance to show the chosen use of the rope.' The dance can be restricted to three or four movements or to movements selected first by the teacher.

4 'Use the rope to tie one part of your body to another. Now pick three basic movements and try to do them tied up. It will change the whole feel of the dance.'

Other Movement Stimuli

The exercises for scarves, ribbons and ropes should give you ideas for other stimuli that could be used. Listed below are some others that I have found useful together with a few ways to use them. The rest I shall leave to you and the children.

Boxes

Wood lasts better than cardboard, but any large box will do.
1 Get inside the boxes. Explore big and small ones, a Jack in the Box, etc.

2 Get on and go round the boxes:
   a Lie on the floor and curve round the box in different ways. Be floppy. This is sometimes a hard concept for children to grasp. Tell them to flop over the box. 'Does it support your weight?'
   b 'What is the opposite of floppy? How can you show that using the box?'

3 Explore the concepts of fast, slow, strong, soft, high and low, using a box.

4 Balancing, expanding and contracting, jumping, rolling and swaying are exciting movements for exploring boxes.

5   Make shapes under, over, around, behind and in front of the boxes. This encourages language development.

Mats

Mats of any size will do.
1   Jumping: on, over, one foot, two feet, with hard or soft energy.

2   Making shapes.

3   Fantasy games; for example, the mats are islands, pools, a castle, a hot spot in the room, etc.

Chairs

1   Crawling under, sliding on stomach over or under.

2   Tunnels.

3   Turned various ways and used for balancing on or for draping the body over.

4   Fantasy: for example, a chair can become a hiding place, a mountain, a boat.

Large Pieces of Material

1   Create environments, such as a dark cave, with pieces of material draped over a table, or a rainbow room with the walls hung with bright colours.

2   Children can move over or under the material while others move it in various ways.

3   With young children, awareness of others can be developed and a lot of fun can be had by using a strong piece of material as a 'magic carpet'. One child lies on the material, while the others stand around the edge and lift him/her. The teacher might need to help. We use magic words or counting for lift off and touchdown.

4   Play more sophisticated versions of 'Peek-a-Boo' using songs. This is good with children who are slow or shy. Use such lines as 'Where is . . . .?', which focuses all the attention on the child. When he/she is found, the song can ask questions such as 'How are you?', 'What do you want to do?', etc. (This idea came from Mozelle Aaron, who used it with success with children with behavioural problems.)

Large Reels

Get these from wood spindles or fishing lines.
1   Use these for rolling activities for the very young. Children roll them from one to another.

2 Use reels for balancing on. Place one of the circular ends of a reel on the ground, step on, and balance. Use two (one for each foot) if necessary. Encourage much 'tarr-rarring' and applause from the audience when someone manages to balance.

3 Do a strongman act using dumbells.

4 Present a circus, using various acts. It doesn't matter if the acts go wrong; the accent can be on flamboyance and carrying things off with aplomb. Of course, the audience must be prepared to enter into the spirit of the thing and support the artists.

Hoops

1 Make shapes inside a hoop; for example, a small shape with one or more people.

2 Play 'horses'. One person has the hoop around her while another (the 'driver') holds on to it. The pair have to travel together making joint decisions about direction and speed.

4 Roll and throw hoops.

5 Fantasy: the hoop can become a hole, a tunnel, a magic ball, a big necklace and many other things.

Foam Boppers

These are clubs made of foam. Use them to:
1 Hit without hurting, have fencing matches, work off aggression.

2 Explore hard and soft energy.

Comments

1 Reverse Garbage centres have many of the objects mentioned in this and other chapters. When you are there, other objects may suggest themselves as movement stimuli. Keep an eye open for interesting objects to use for dance everywhere you go.

2 Always allow the children to explore objects for themselves and, if possible, have a time when very little direction is given. Stay at the side of the room and watch what the children do, not only in movement, but in social interaction as well. I've learned a lot about children this way and I can also see what skills they need to work on in the more formal part of the movement lesson. Often see how to tackle teaching that formal part, too. I might see that the children need greater awareness of each other, so I develop an exercise based on the way the children were playing together spontaneously. With young children it becomes free play with the objects given and it can

appear mundane to the teacher. Don't worry about that. The children are often fulfilling needs that the teacher hasn't noticed. Once I couldn't understand why one bright inner city class ran round and round the big hall with whatever stimuli they were given; it seemed far below their creative level. However, when I looked at their home and school environments, which were spatially restricted, I realised that there was very little space for them to run in their everyday lives. They needed to run. After that I included fun, fast-running activities at the beginning of every lesson, with the result that the class was better controlled and the children more alert.

3   Don't let lack of stimuli stump you. If you can't get to Reverse Garbage, use what's around the school, including chairs, tables, benches, trees, doors, walls, etc. This helps the children to see their environment in a different light.

4   The exercises suggested for a specific object need not necessarily be used for that object; some of the exercises written for ropes, for example, could be done with a stick or a piece of material.

5   Any activities that are made into dance pieces by the children should be shown to the rest of the class, from a starting position and finishing with a freeze.

6   Materials can of course be combined: hoops can be placed on or in boxes; ropes can be tied to chairs or hoops.

chapter 5:   mask work

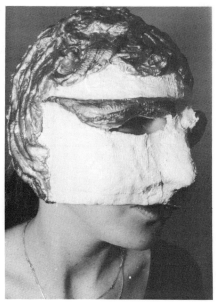

Half masks.

Young girls can play out their fantasies about being beautiful.

Introduction

The information in this section is fairly detailed and caters for children from kindergarten to Year 6. Some of the work shows long-term aims and achievements, while other exercises achieve more instant results. Choose what suits you and your class best, after having a look at the whole chapter.

Being able to make the mask look alive is called 'carrying' the mask. It is achieved by changing the body to suit the mask, making big, bold movements and holding moments of stillness. The voice needs also to be changed if speech is used. It should be exciting to see the children learn to carry the mask. Don't be put off if results are not fantastic at first. Inhibitions are quickly lost with masks.

Development depends on the child being aware that he can become a different person or creature behind the mask. His viewpoint changes as the character. This is achieved by the ritual of putting on and taking off the mask (see 'Mask Work Procedure' on page 61) and by the teacher's belief in the situation being created (see 'Principles of Mask Work' below).

The power of imagination and the degree to which we can control our viewpoint of the world are most important in mask work. And the mask, because it totally changes the appearance, is a very strong medium for bringing out all kinds of hidden areas within ourselves. I have called the teacher the 'director'

54

for these exercises, as mask work can't be taught, only explored. This is because there is no particular, cut and dried way to act when you are exploring a mask. Three children might use the same mask, one after the other, but each of them will use different body movements, sounds, etc. and will create a different character from the others'. Especially in the early stages of mask work, the teacher must encourage the child's own creativity rather than imposing her ideas. (This does not necessarily apply, however, to directing a performance piece.)

So, for mask work, you can initiate a whole new world of people and happenings in your classroom, then sit back and enjoy the fun.

Principles of Mask Work

1   The mask is a catalyst which transforms the wearer into another person or object.
2   As another being, the wearer sees the world through the eyes of the mask character, not through his own, everyday eyes.
3   The change of character takes place the moment the mask is put on the face and ceases as soon as the mask is removed. This dividing line must be clearly upheld by the director.
4   The mask must be treated with respect, both physically and verbally.
5   As soon as the mask is on, the character is addressed by his mask's name, not by his usual name.
6   The director must at all times show in voice, choice of language and emotion that she totally believes in the fantasy that she is creating.
7   The mask is larger than life. Use big shapes, moments of stillness and stylisation.
8   Masks can be used to aid various educational aims. They can also explore language and concepts such as tall and small and colours, and abstracts such as emotions. This is more clearly outlined in 'Mask Work Procedure' and 'Further Ideas for Mask Work' on pages 61 and 68.

Types of Masks and How to Make Them

It is best to augment this section with books on mask making from libraries, etc.

Masks do not have to be life-like; they can symbolise or suggest the character you want. The merest suggestion of a mask can change the whole face, as can the Pierrot or Party Hat below.

Pierrot mask.

Pierrot or Party Hat

False noses, beards, glasses and wigs can create whole new characters. They are easy to make or cheap to buy if you do not have time or cannot make your own masks. They can be applied to many of the exercises given in this chapter.

Hand-Made Paper Masks

There are basically two types of mask: full face and half face. Choose the type that suits your purposes best.

The total transformation provided by a full-face mask gives the child more anonymity.

Full and half face monster masks.

Performer's face

The half-face mask is better for speaking, since the voice becomes muffled under a full mask. The half-face mask makes the child work more because the lower face can still be seen and has to take on the characteristics of the mask on the upper face.

Experiment yourself. I am listing only masks which I have found to work well. Try other materials and types of mask. This is still a very experimental area. I have only given a few ideas.

Papier mâché: I hardly mention this medium because I find it slow, cumbersome and often disastrous. There is, however, a variation of the papier mâché method using glue and tissue paper which I mention below.

Masks can be made from cartridge, cardboard, drawing paper or any other type of paper that has some thickness. The shape of the mask is drawn on the paper and put against the face for eyes, etc., to be marked for cutting out. String or elastic is attached to the sides by staples or through reinforced holes. Paper hair can be added, as can paint, glitter, etc.

Comments

1   These masks are weak and do not last long, but they are good for experimenting with different characters and ideas. Reinforcement can be done by soaking tissue paper (toilet paper is great) in a 50/50 mixture of water soluble wood glue and water and putting a layer or two of this over the paper mask. It will dry to plastic hardness.

2   Do not stick on too much hair or other additions since they tear the mask.

3   These masks do not always fit well and tend to slip off.

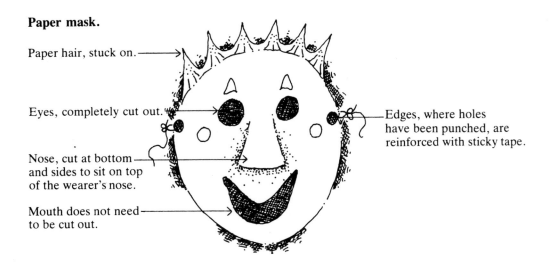

Paper mask.

Paper hair, stuck on.

Eyes, completely cut out.

Nose, cut at bottom and sides to sit on top of the wearer's nose.

Mouth does not need to be cut out.

Edges, where holes have been punched, are reinforced with sticky tape.

Paper Bags

Big supermarket bags can slip over the whole head. Again, as with other paper masks, care is needed to get the eye holes in the right place: some kind of re-inforcement could be done to make these more durable.

Paper Bag Mask.

More Durable Masks: Plaster Bandage

The most successful way I have found of making long-lasting masks is by using plaster impregnated bandage. Its brand name is 'Gypsona' and it can be got at any chemist, but more cheaply and in bulk at surgical suppliers. Normally it is used for setting broken limbs. Three layers of this material, used in the method described below, make a light-weight durable mask.

A mould is needed. A wig stand (with a face), a cheap Star Wars or spider Man plastic mask, or the child's own face can be used. (I've done most of my masks on the childrens faces — it gives the best fit). Whatever you use must be covered with vaseline or cold cream first. Then layers are built up out of strips of bandage cut about 10 centimetres long. (Some around the eyes and nose need to be smaller than 10 centimetres.)

Breathing and eye holes must be left. Cut up your roll of bandage beforehand, and have a wide container of water and plenty of tissues and towels handy. Cover the person, if you are using a live mould, so that he/she does not get wet. I usually use a large garbage bag. I cut off a strip from the open end to act as a protective headband. Cut a hole in the other end of the head and pull over body.

Applying plaster bandage.

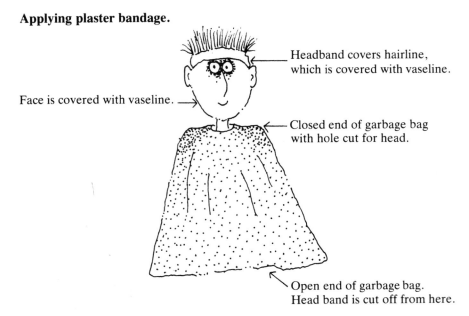

Headband covers hairline, which is covered with vaseline.

Face is covered with vaseline.

Closed end of garbage bag with hole cut for head.

Open end of garbage bag. Head band is cut off from here.

Method

1   Start at the forehead. Dunk bandage in water, keeping it flat, and remove immediately from water. Shake off excess moisture. Place on the forehead.

2   Work down the face carefully, leaving big eyeholes and breathing holes if it is to be a full-face mask.

3   Drips will occur and perhaps run down the neck. This can be minimised by having the bandage wet but not sopping, and by lying the child down.

4   Each piece of bandage must overlap the ones next to it, as shown below.

5   Do three layers.

6   Allow 5–10 minutes to dry on the face or 24 hours on a mould.

7   Get the child to screw up his/her face to loosen the mask and remove it gently.

8   Bind the edges and check for weak spots that might need extra bandage. The edges are bound by folding a strip of wet bandage over them. Do this around the eyes too.

Part of a mask, showing how bandage pieces overlap.

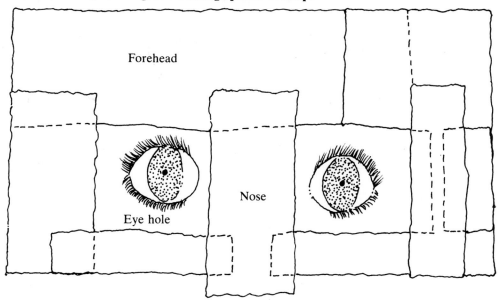

- - - - Bandage covered by overlapping piece.

9 Features can be built up with extra bandage, or tissue paper covered with bandage. Fix them securely to the mask by laying a couple of layers of bandage over the top, leaving plenty of bandage securing the paper to the original mask.

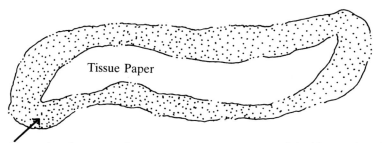

Plaster bandage over tissue paper secures paper to original layer of mask.

10 The mask can be finished with a layer of tissue paper soaked in 50/50 solution of water soluble wood glue and water, put on like papier mâché, for a durable, plastic-coated finish. Otherwise it can be painted and varnished. Appendages made of paper, material, etc., are very effective.

11 Punch holes and put elastic in to hold the mask on the face.

Large, simple shapes are most effective in mask work.

Comments

1 Children feel personally involved if masks are made on their faces.

2 'Gypsona' is rather expensive, but four masks could be made for the use of the whole class if you use the audience techniques listed under 'Mask Activities' on page 64.

3 One child can put the bandage on another's face, unless the children are very young. In the process they learn to care for each other especially if they know that the person they are plastering will in turn plaster them!

4 Plastic wood can be used on a mould instead of Gypsona. Do not use plastic wood on the face — it takes longer to dry than Gypsona.

Mask Work Procedure

Introduction

1 This procedure can be used at any primary school level, as long as the language is appropriate, and for any of the given topics in this chapter.

2 Do not neglect to take time to talk the children into and out of the mask. They need strong barriers to know when they are their character (when the mask goes on the face) and when to stop being their character (when the mask is taken off).

3 Respect their characters.

4 Do not use children's real names when talking to them in mask. Use the name of the mask, or say 'Paul's creature' or 'John's creature', never 'Paul' or 'John'.

5 If the children want to ask you a question and they are wearing the mask, they either ask you as their character or take off the mask.

6 I have outlined some of the following exercises in the way I would actually speak them to a class, step by step. I have used the idea of a creature and his world for the first series of exercises below; however it can be adapted to other ideas which are listed later. So, if the following exercises do not suit your needs, look at 'Further Ideas' on page 68.

EXERCISE 17 Putting on the Mask

a 'Sit in a space.'
b 'Close your eyes and put a room or a box around you.' (See space exercises, pages 10–17. I sometimes use a relaxation exercise here. 'Be in your own space.'
c 'Open your eyes but stay in your own space. Pretend you are the only person in the room.'

d   'Take your mask, hold it face up and look at it. Say "Hello Mask. I am going to be you".' (Depending on age group, children say this out loud or to themselves.)

e   'See what kind of creature you are going to be.' (Perhaps give some suggestions: tall, small, strong, weak, happy, sad, angry, loving, sly or open.)

f   'Keep the mask in front of you; close your eyes and see your creature standing in front of you, as if you're watching a film.' (You might not want to use the word 'creature'. Choose language that suits your children.)

g   'Look at the face of your creature (keep your eyes closed) in the picture in your mind — the face is like the mask you were looking at. See it in your mind.'

h   'See in your mind what its arms look like, what its body looks like, its legs and feet. What is it wearing? How does it stand?'

i   'Now, in your mind picture, make the creature walk. How does it walk?' (Bent over, tall, heavily, softly, bandy legs, knock-kneed. You might like to get them to lead with one body part — see comments at the end of this chapter).

j   'Open your eyes, look at the mask and put it on.'

k   'Stand up in your space. There is no one else in the room except you. If you see another body look through it — its not there.'

l   'Make a statue to show me what your new creature's body is like. How does it stand? Hold its arms? What position are its legs in?'

m 'Make the statue big and clear so I can really see what kind of thing you are.'

EXERCISE 18 Moving

a   'Walk round the room as your creature. How does it walk? Remember there is no-one else in the room.'

b   'Stop, make a statue. Big . . . clear. Hold it!' (Even if the creature is small and weak the statue must be clear and exaggerated.)

c   Repeat a and b several times.

EXERCISE 19 Landscapes

Now a series of activities can be developed to suit whatever you are particularly trying to direct the children to discover about their character (see point 8 in 'Principles of Mask Work', page 54.) If you want a general exploration of the character, carry on as follows. If not, there are more specific exercises for language, emotions, etc., listed in 'Further Ideas for Mask Work' on page 68.

a   'Find your spot in the room and go to it.'

b   'Curl up but do not take off your mask.'

c   'Close your eyes, creatures, and get a mind picture of the kind of country that you live in. It could have blue trees and purple rocks or be totally different from anything on this planet.'

d   'In the picture see your creature moving through its world.'
e   'What is it doing?'
f   'Stand up, alone. The room has changed into your world, the world of your creature. When you open your eyes everything will be as it is in your world.'
g   'Open your eyes and begin, alone, to move around your world.'
h   'Stop, make a statue to show what you think about your world.'
i   'Put out your hands. There is something of your world in front of you. Run your hands over it find out the shape, colour, feel, smell. What do you do with it? Can you eat it? Sit on it? Is it hard or soft?' (It is best if children create the illusion of their object in thin air, rather than using an actual object.)
j   'Make a statue to show what you think of it. Strong and clear.'
k   'Make a sound to show what you think of it.'
l   Repeat i with different imaginary objects.
m   'Now find something to eat. What is it?'
n   'How do you eat?' (It doesn't have to be human way of eating.)
o   'Now find what part of your world you live in. Where is your home? Do you build your home or is it a natural part of your world?'
p   'Go home.'
q   'Find where you sleep in your home. Find your sleeping position and go to sleep.'
r   See 'Landscapes', on page 89 for other ideas in this area.

EXERCISE 20   Interaction between Characters.

a   'Now your world has some other creatures in it.'
b   'Wake up and look around. Just look and see all the other creatures.'
c   'Catch one creature's eye. When I say, "go", get up and have a look at it. Do not touch the other creature's body. There is a rule in this land that creatures may not touch.'
d   'Make a statue to show what you think of the creature you have met.'
e   'Have a conversation with it in creature language.'
f   Let an improvisation develop. If arguments or fights develop, that's all right. Insist on no body contact. Masks do not touch, it spoils the effect when they get too close. Fights take place by sounds, waving of arms, huge dramatic blows that stop short of the body and mock stranglings that take place 10 centimetres or further away from the throat. Children enjoy this when they realise that they can be more aggressive when they don't have to worry about hurting others.

EXERCISE 21   Action and Reaction

Mask characters are encouraged to act and react towards each other and their environment.
a   'Go and explore the room/landscape together.'

b 'Go and show your partner round your world — then swap.'
c Go and perform some activity together; for example:
ask another couple for something;
get food;
scare another group;
build a shelter;
go on a journey across the misty mountains, or whatever (fraught with danger of course).
d Use freezes, statues, big shapes, etc., for the children to show clearly their reactions to the adventures. Encourage slowness and clarity.

EXERCISE 22   Using an Audience

An audience can be an important part of mask work if used properly. It gives the children an opportunity to see the masks in action on other people and encourages clarity and moments of stillness. It enables the children to understand when a character is really taking a person over and the mask is really being carried. Failure to 'carry' the mask becomes obvious to an audience when you just see a person with a mask on instead of the new and different character which is created when a mask takes over the whole body.

I get children to watch each other in mask frequently. It also gives me a chance to enjoy seeing individuals work and give more detailed comments if I should wish to.

Any of the exercises so far described could be done by one of the children while the others watch. Or you might like to do some of the improvisations listed in Exercise 24 (page 65). A good start to audience work is:

a The performer goes out of class or behind a screen and puts on his mask. He greets the mask out of sight of the audience.
b When he is ready he peers around the door or screen at the audience.
c Then he enters with his character's special way of moving.
d The performer makes a shape and perhaps a sound when he gets to the centre of the performance space.
e The director asks the character a question, such as 'Where do you live? What is your name? What did you eat for breakfast?' The child must answer as the mask.
f He then leaves as he came and takes off the mask, thanking it, outside the door or behind the screen.
g The performer without mask then bows to the audience, who acknowledges him with applause. A supportive audience is most necessary so that children can feel safe. You can set the tone by the way you react to the masks yourself.

EXERCISE 23 Improvisations for an Audience

a Character **A** enters and begins doing something very simple (for example, sits down, sweeps the floor, eats, sleeps).
b After a few moments Character **B** enters and discovers Character **A** by looking from a distance, then going closer.
c Improvisation takes place.
d Stop the action after a suitable time by freezing the performers.

More complex improvisations could be built up and used as the basis for a public or assembly performance piece.
a Character **A** enters and performs simple task.
b Character **B** enters, observes and makes a statue to show his reaction.
c Improvisation.
d Character **A** leaves.
e Character **B** is alone.
f Character **C** enters, observes, reacts.
g Characters **B** and **C** interact.
h Character **B** leaves, and so on.

Alternatively: as for points a and b above, when characters **A** and **B** are interacting, Character **C** comes on and watches them, then reacts from a distance, then joins them. The three characters interact, then a fourth comes on, and so on. No-one leaves. This is more chaotic, but it can be fun. Especially good visually are statues and freezes which are added at strategic points.

EXERCISE 24 Ending the Lesson

It does not matter how many of the exercises here are covered in one lesson, but at the end of every lesson the mask must be formally put aside. This prevents the children hanging on to energy or viewpoints left over from the mask.

a 'Sit down in a space and take off your mask.'
b 'Hold it face up and really look at it.'
c 'The mask has enabled you to be a creature (or whatever), a different person. Now it is time to put your creature away and go back to being the you that does other things, reading, playing, eating lunch, laughing, getting angry and all the other things you do in the everyday world. So put the creature away so that you can get on with other things. Look at the mask, brush the energy off your face back into the mask and say "Thank you, mask".' (This need not be said aloud by older children.)
d 'Now push the mask away from you and stand up.'
e 'Shake your hands at the mask with a sound. Shake your feet with a sound, shake your head, etc. Shake your whole body with a sound.'

Note: If the mask is taken on and off several times during one lesson, as can often be the case, it is best for children to say a quick but sincere 'Hello' and

'Thank you' each time, so that the barriers between mask and non-mask are clear. The longer ritual of sitting down with the mask and putting the energy back into the mask is only done at the beginning and end of each class. Even with older children a few moments spent looking at the mask before and after putting it on enhances the character change and reverence for the mask.

Comments on Exercises

When a teacher directs mask work, she must be responsible for making sure that the children leave the lesson in good shape. That is, that they leave their characters behind in the mask, are not confused about who or where they are and are not frightened or disorientated. With emotionally disturbed children I take special care and usually do a few extra closing exercises.

Special Exercises to Dissociate from the Mask

EXERCISE 25

a   'Look at the mask. Who is it? What is its name?'
b   'Look at yourself. Who are you? What is your name?'
c   Repeat until answers are crisp and sure. The child can just look at the mask then at himself without answering the questions, if you feel that is better.

EXERCISE 26

Make each command clearly, confidently and precisely.

a   'Look at the wall.' (Point to wall. When the children have finished looking at the wall, they look back at you.)
b   To acknowledge their carrying out the command, when they are looking back at you, you say, 'Thank you.'
c   'Look at the ceiling.' (Point.)
d   'Thank you.'
e   'Look at the floor.' (Point.)
f   'Thank you.'

EXERCISE 27

Let the child take you round the room showing you objects, telling you what they are and touching them.

EXERCISE 28

a   Get the children to run to different parts of the room and touch them, look at them, smell them and feel them.
b   Adjust the language and activities of the mask work to suit your class. For kindergarten or prep. children, they would need to be greatly simplified.

Perhaps finding the walk, sound and a sleeping place for the creature might be enough for them. Later you could go on to a meeting between two masks and a small performance in front of the class. With older children whole, complicated landscapes can be built up in the imagination and explored by the masks (see Landscapes, page 89).

c   Any number of exercises can be done per lesson, depending on the children's attention span. Exercises can also be repeated using the same or different characters and circumstances. Repetition will cause the children to develop their characters more.

d   When older children are familiar with the procedure for sitting down and getting into the mask at the beginning of the lesson, they can do it in their own time without you talking them through it. However, be sure they don't rush it when doing it by themselves but sit quietly, getting into communication with the mask and seeing their character in their mind's eye.

e   During a session a mask character might begin to develop a very strong personality which might not always be nice. Whenever possible, let the character become what it will (providing it doesn't actually hurt bodies).

f   Be sparing in your comments — in fact you don't have to comment at all. 'Thank you. Next creature, please,' is enough. There is no right or wrong, only different characters. Children can become abusive or angry during a mask improvisation. As long as they don't touch, let the masks handle it and watch the reactions of one mask to another. See if the child suddenly loses his mask character and becomes himself again because of fear or aggression. If a child comes out of his mask character and starts acting as himself, it is probably best to stop the improvisation.

g   Stress to the children that once they say goodbye to the masks they do not bring up events created by the mask; for example, 'You said "bloody" when you had your mask on, that's rude', or 'You looked stupid with your mask on, yrkk!' or 'You called me fatty when you had your mask on, now say you're sorry'. The event finishes when the mask is taken off. If something is unresolved and the children can't seem to forget it, let them put their masks back on and let the masks solve it.

h   To encourage children to move differently, ask them as their creature to find a body part to lead them as they move. For example, they could stick out an elbow in front of them and let the elbow lead them round the space, altering the way the whole body moves. They could stick out their stomachs or lead with a knee, causing a dragging effect. Sideways movements could be led with the hip or ribs, and one finger sticking out in front would create a strange creature. You could give a lesson on this beforehand and work at different levels. (This idea comes from Helen Zigmond.)

Further Ideas for Mask Work

Opposites

Use masks to show opposites or differences; for example, tall, small, differentiation between colours, wide, narrow, etc.

Have a variety of masks in different colours. Perhaps red, white, green and brown. Four would do for the whole class. It would be good to design them to show the characteristics they were to represent: a tall red mask, a small white mask, a wide green mask, and a narrow brown mask. However, it does not matter if all the masks are the same shape. Once the masks have been bought or made and the theme decided on, then agreement must be reached about what the masks represent. The children will have individual feelings about the masks and what they represent to them. These need to be taken into account, along with the general decisions made as a class. Of course, the words you use, the design of the mask and the theme is up to you and the children. You could have four masks of different colours for emotions or tone levels. A pink mask becomes a shy person; a black mask is a hard, cold aloof person; a yellow mask is a warm outgoing person; and a light blue mask becomes a bored, frustrated person. There are many themes you can choose and colours are not the only way of denoting mask type — size, shape, expression, type of material, etc. can also be used.

1   Reinforce concepts of tall and small, colours, number and language in this exciting way for Kindergarten and Prep.

2   With infants, experiment with body shapes and contrasts of character: the tall pirate meets the small old man, for example.

3   Older children can put concepts together and perhaps use scarves, ribbons or other accessories to denote extra qualities; for example, the character wears a red mask, which means she is tall and a black scarf round her waist to show that she is thin. Another character wears a white mask denoting smallness and a yellow scarf denoting fatness. Thus you can have an improvisation of a tall thin woman meeting a small fat man.

The children must know what the masks and scarves represent. A wall chart could be useful to help them remember. Once characters have been chosen then the exercises given in Mask Work Procedure can be done entirely or partially. Always get the children into and out of the mask using the proper procedures: creating a mind picture and thanking the mask at the end. Stories can be made up about the characters too.

Characters

Masks can be life-like or representational creations of a person from literature, history or current affairs. The child can do most of the Mask Procedure exercises as his character, getting an insight into the life, times and viewpoint of the person. This is an exciting way to explore history, make a story come to life or be that pop star or hero you always wanted to be. As well as doing the exercises already given, the characters can come out and tell you about themselves, interact with other characters and make up plays or dances.

Creatures

These have already been mentioned, but it's worth saying that making creature masks can be fun, as anything goes.

Animals

Becoming animals can be effective if the children really look at body shape, sounds and the movements of the particular animal they want to be. At Prep. or kindergarten it's fairly basic: kangaroo jumps with two feet together, limbs hang in front. Older children can observe much more subtle things, especially if they go to the zoo or watch a film. For example, when walking a lion changes direction by crossing one front paw over the other. What is a horse's foot pattern when galloping? What's a canter? How does a fish change direction when swimming?

Emotions

Emotions can be suggested by the line of the mouth, eyebrows, etc. These expressions can be stylised or life-like. Behind the mask the child feels at liberty to explore socially unacceptable emotions safely, so do not judge. The emotion should be taken into the whole body, changing posture, walk and muscular tension. See if an emotion opens or closes the body; that is, whether there is an outflow of energy or a holding in of energy. For anger, for instance, the body is upright or slightly leaned forward and there is an outflow of energy. Apathy or depression cause the body to slouch down, slack and closed, and energy does not flow out.

Basic Movements

If the children know the basic movements (see Chapter 2), get them to work on a movement piece in mask. This can be most effective. Give or let them choose three movements (which can be added to) for their character to do. They must use the body posture, way of moving and viewpoint of their character. Experiment with sounds too.

It becomes interesting when two different characters make a dance together. Then the movements, direction, mood and floor pattern of the dance can show the inter-relation of the two characters. For example, how would Peter and the Wolf relate to each other using run, jump and big shape? Some excellent performance pieces can be developed using this method.

Stories

When working on stories, allow the characters to improvise, as well as stick to the story; you might develop some amusing variations.

Outdoors

Characters can go and explore the outside world — the playground, park, street or any other suitable area.

Ideas for Performance

Mask is a very effective medium for public performance of any kind. Ideas can come from:

1   Improvisations which are cleaned up, exaggerated and stylised, then practiced and polished.

2   Enacting a story, using readers to tell the story whilst the mask characters act it out, perhaps using some lines. The characters must be larger than life.

3   Choreographed movement pieces — see Basic Movements on page 69.

Hints on Performance

1   Use big, or clear, small shapes and exaggerate and stylise.

2   Use lots of moments of stillness and statues.

3   See that the performers look at the audience or the back wall of the performance space and share whatever they do with the audience.

chapter 6: fantasy: using mental pictures

Matthew (Year 6) wrote part of the script for the play, too!

Introduction

The conscious and controlled use of fantasy develops the imagination, encourages movement and language and enables the child to experience other viewpoints.

The child must be able to start, create and stop the fantasy at will. Uncontrolled, unconscious flipping into fantasy can cause problems. By consciously creating fantasies the child gains control of his creative abilities.

It is important when working with mental pictures to:

1   Be in the fantasy oneself, by creating the mental picture in your own mind then passing it on to the children by your tone of voice, enthusiasm, and commitment to the illusion.

2   Use relaxation exercises before and after, when necessary.

3   Get the children into present time after the fantasy; that is, make sure that they are back in the present world of classroom and aware of this moment, not still being wizards, or lions or still feeling emotions created by the fantasy.

4   Make the reality they return to after the fantasy pleasant.

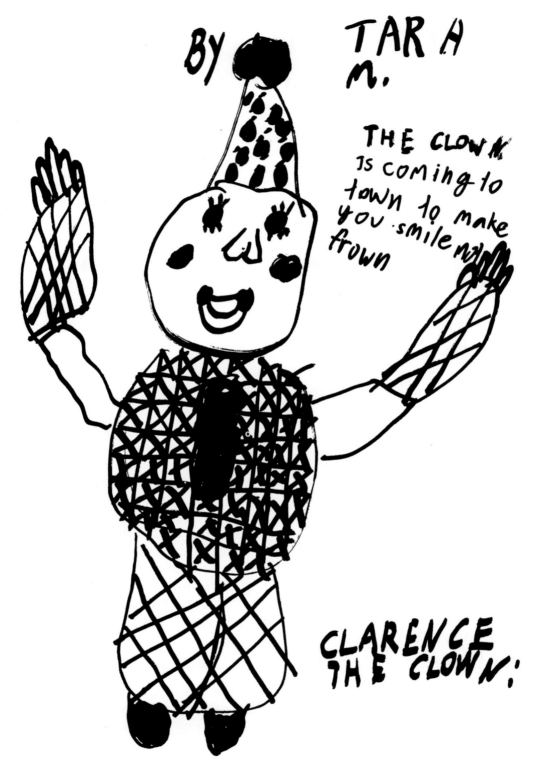

BY

TARA M.

THE CLOWN Is coming to town to make you smile no frown

CLARENCE THE CLOWN:

One day we dressed up and found out how our clowns walked, ran, swayed, turned, etc.

This Martian clown helped Dimitri bring out the zany side of his nature.

Sky played a convict in the end of term play. The ball and chain obviously made a great impression.

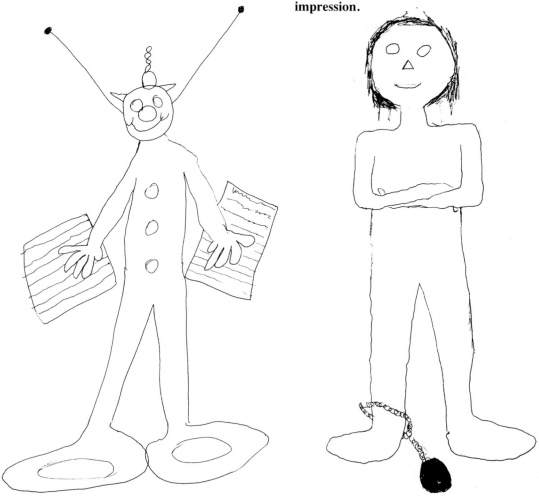

5   Treat the power of fantasy seriously, to validate the work done by the children and to allow them to see that the creation of mind pictures is a valuable part of their make-up.

6   Develop their fantasy-work by using other mediums — creative writing, drama, music and painting can all be enhanced by using the exercises that follow, and many of the themes can make lovely subjects for painting, writing, etc. Whole topics can be explored on many levels.

7   Enjoy it.

8   Talk the children through step by step in a controlled manner. Be aware of the necessity for this.

9   Make your commentary relevant to the class you are taking. Use language, energy and concepts that you know will suit them.

10 Get a mental picture of something by creating not only the shape but the mass, size, texture, smell, taste, colour and mood of the object pictured.

Very young children can not create such complex fantasies as older ones. However all these exercises can be adapted to suit. See the comment at the end of Space Journey, page 94.

Mitchell's wizard (Year 4).

Mental Pictures: Energy

The Wizard

(See also Exercise 12 on page 24.)

I usually do this piece early on in the programme, as soon as they have enough control of space to do it. It gives them experience in several principles of creative movement which I will state in brackets in the outline below.

1   Relaxation on the floor (see pages 99 and 101). The teacher then begins to talk the children through the exercise.

2   'Now your body is going to change from your everyday body into a wizard's body. When you feel the touch of the magic scarf (or whatever else you want to use), you will fill up with wizard's power. The power that can change things, the power that can make spells. Stay very still and feel your body fill with power. Feel it. Feel it in your head, your arms, your finger tips, your chest, your legs, etc.' (Awareness of body)

3   'There is a special law about wizards' power. If you look at or speak to anyone else the magic power will disappear for a moment. Your power is strongest when you work alone.' (Self control, awareness of personal space)

4   (Some musical accompaniment might begin here.)
    'Stand up, stand at centre, very still. Find a spot on the wall and look at it. Lift one arm, feel the power in that arm, point at the spot you are looking at and let all that power in your arm flow out and hit that spot on the wall (with a sound). Let that power, your wizard's power, change that spot on the wall to anything you like. Put a picture on that spot of whatever you like and look at the picture.' (Ability to create mental pictures)

5   a   Give the same commands using different parts of the body to create the pictures and different parts of the room to put them in. For example power from the head to create a picture on the ceiling (with a sound). Power from the chest (expand chest, open front of body) to create a picture on a spot on the wall. Power from the foot to create a picture on the floor. Talk the children through each step as in 4. Use an expressive tone of voice. Encourage opening up, expansion and lightness of the body parts used. Other body parts that can be used are the stomach, knee, elbow, back and ear. Isolations can get even more subtle if you use knuckles, neck, hip etc.

    b   If the children need suggestions for mental pictures then make it a lot of fun. Flowers can grow out of walls, elephants can swing from lightbulbs and lions can appear out of the floor. The mental picture must be put on the wall, ceiling or floor as clearly as possible.

    c   The idea is to cover as much of the room as possible. Pictures are superimposed, each on a different point of the room. It doesn't matter which body part is aimed at the point in the room.

    d   Remember that as well as mental pictures, this exercise aims at awareness of personal energy (power). Feel the energy come up through the body, leave via the appropriate body part, connect and create a mental picture at that spot.

6   Once the children have got the idea of awareness of exterior points, awareness of personal energy and connecting the two via a part of the body to create a mental picture, you can then say, 'Go all around the room changing points anywhere in the room.' (Use sound). Watch, encourage and stay part of the fantasy during this time.

7   When they have had enough, say, 'Freeze, sink down onto the floor and rest.'

8   'Soon, wizard, we are going to need the room for something else. The mental pictures are great but they might get in the way when we want to do something else so now we are going to make all the pictures disappear. When I say "Go", jump up and find a movement to get rid of all the spells that you have made around the room. Find a movement to make the pictures disappear and clean up the room. Stand up, go!' (Flicking or dabbing — some quick body movement — is needed here.) Encourage fast, uncontrolled movements all over the room, as a contrast to the slow, controlled movements of the first part of the exercise. This also enables children to realise that fantasies, once created, need to be stopped and the 'real' world created again. They are in conscious control of the illusion. To reinforce this, use different music from the first part.

9   'Make sure there are no pictures left anywhere in the room.'

10   'Sink down on the floor and rest.'

11   Do a body awareness, relaxation exercise to help the children get in touch with their bodies again.

12   'Now slowly sit up.'

13   Get the children to look at the different parts of the room, but this time without the identity of the wizard. Make your commands clear, sharp and precise and point to that part of the room as you give the command. (See Exercise 26, page 66, for a detailed outline of this exercise.)

14   Check, by looking, that the children are back in present time.

by Natalie Julita

78

Comments

1 This exercise needs explicit instructions and control. You can achieve this by talking the children through step by step.

2 Music: I use Tangerine Dream's 'Rubicon'. Any powerful piece will do for the spells section. Then for cleaning up I use a light, lively piece played by pan flute and organ.

3 Make this exercise your own by finding wording that suits your class.

4 This exercise enables children to imagine — to see with other eyes and to become someone else. This is necessary for any creative work — painting, writing or drama. It aids sensitivity and the ability to see other points of view.

The Gift

'The Wizard' is concerned with energy transferred to objects. 'The Gift' is concerned with energy transferred to people. The child's awareness of space now includes other people, whereas in 'The Wizard' the children were asked to be aware only of themselves.

Talk the children through this exercise. I have not done this in the directions given below, so create your own dialogue.

1 Each child sits in a space and is given a scarf (ribbon or whatever).

2 Ask the child to look at the scarf and to change it, with a mental picture, into something special that he would like to have. It can be anything from the Opera House to a rabbit. A tambourine or something to wave or shake over each person's scarf or some magic words can help to create the picture and make the transformation.

3 Go round and ask each child what he has changed his scarf into.

4 Tell the children that their special things can be shared with others.

5 Demonstrate by picking up your scarf, holding it draped over your extended arms. Get up and begin to walk round the room, keeping the children in view.

6 Tell the children that you will give your special thing to someone who looks as though he/she really wants it. As you walk, make energy flow out from your whole body, including the face and hands. Walk slowly, so that you are aware of everyone and they are aware of you. The mood is expectant.

Scarf

7   When as 'giver' you find the person to whom you want to give your special thing, you go over and give him/her the scarf, still being aware of everyone.

8   The recipient puts down the gift scarf, picks up his/her own special thing and begins to carry it round the room, giving out energy and receiving it from the expectant faces and bodies of the others. This procedure continues until everyone has had a go.

Comments

1   Encourage openess of face, arms and chest, with no tension in the shoulders or arms, so that energy can flow.

2   Be aware of the feeling in the room whilst this exercise is going on. I've often found it to be quite special.

3   This exercise can develop children's awareness of their own specialness and uniqueness.

4   I sometimes use background music — classical, Jonathan Livingston Seagull, Neil Diamond, Chariots of Fire by Vagelis.

The Basic Movements and Mental Pictures

As well as being developed in the ways described in Chapter 3, the basic movements can also be taught through fantasy work. Here I will give examples of fantasy pieces and state the basic movements used. They are, of course, combined with the use of time, space and energy. I have not dealt with all the basic movements but I hope that the exercises given here will be a springboard for you and the children to create your own.

Walking

I have already mentioned the idea of selecting one part of the body to lead you round the room, as a way of developing unusual movements.

1   Lie down and do a relaxation exercise.

2   'At the touch of the magic scarf (or whatever) on your face, your body will be able to change into a different shape. One part of your body will stick out, an elbow or a knee, stomach or chin — whatever part you want.'

3   'Get up and see which part of your body is going to stick out. How does it change your size and shape?'

4   'Move around the room with that part of your body leading. What direction do you move in — backwards, forwards, sideways or diagonally? Does the leading body part slow you down or speed you up? Does the way you move give you an emotion or mood?

5 'Sink down to the floor and rest.'

6 Repeat from 2 to 5, directing that another body part be found. Repeat several times, finding different body shapes, speeds and levels each time.

7 Of course, children can also make sounds, meetings between creatures occur, etc.

8 Paintings and stories can be done about 'my creature' or 'one day I woke up and my body moved differently!'

9 Music: anything that is at a walking pace and is a little weird with a variety of moods.

Running

To explore different types of running you could perhaps have an everyday situation; for example, being late for school. The children can:

1 run out of the house and out the gate;

2 run down the road;

3 run through a puddle;

4 run through some mud;

5 run round an old lady;

6 bump into someone;

7 run across the road (look first, and go down and up curbs);

8 run round the corner;

9 fall over;

10 arrive at the school gate.

11 The children finish story for themselves: was he late? Had the bell gone? Had he made a mistake and come to school on the weekend? Because the children will have different routes when they themselves come to school, it is best to decide on a common child and a common route for all the children to try.

12 Choose music to fit the hurrying mood, such as the 'Flight of the Bumble Bee', parts of the 'William Tell Overture' or 'Night on a Bald Mountain'.

Crawling

Develop a fantasy for crawling by talking about occasions on which adults or children might crawl. The children might suggest that people crawl when they are hurt or when they don't want to be seen.

1 The scene is the American Wild West.

2 Children in pairs are suitably spaced. There are no touching bodies throughout this piece.

3 Have a quick, traditional, Wild West shootout.

4 Both children are wounded and fall down, holding the wounded part.

5 They must leave the scene before the sheriff arrives but are afraid to stand because of their wounds and for fear that the other might shoot.

6 They attempt to crawl away quickly and unobtrusively, taking into account the body part that is wounded. How do you crawl if you've been shot in the arm, leg or stomach? How will that effect the speed at which you move and the shape of your body?

7 An effective performance piece can be made out of this if it is controlled enough. Children can ham it up as much as they like.

8   Perhaps restrict the children to one shot each in the gunfight — they must aim at a part of their opponent's body and fire. The opponent looks at the other child's arm and that directs for him the part of his body that is wounded. He receives the shot, reacts, holds the shot body part and falls over, after aiming and firing at his opponent himself. This is a creative and effective way to avoid a riot of shooting and shouting.

9   The children will appreciate the indulgence of the teacher who has been part of a fantasy that is often used in their everyday play. They are often surprised and pleased to be allowed to use fantasies that are usually frowned upon by adults in schools.

10 Be prepared to join in. It really breaks down the children's inhibitions.

11 Music: anything from films or epics that's appropriate, such as 'Big Country' or the folk song 'Streets of Lorado'.

Big and Small Shapes

These lend themselves to many fantasy situations. The following activity is one that enables children to play with energy:

1   'Stand at centre.'

2   'Imagine that there is a big bag around you. Stand very still and create the feeling of a big bag that completely covers you. It's quite a heavy bag and you can feel it all over you.' (You could vary this by having one or more children be the bag around the other child.)

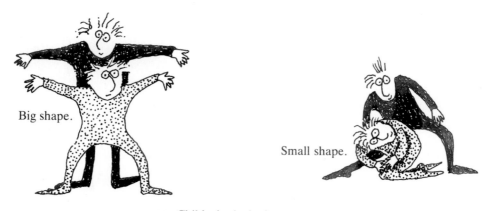

Big shape.

Small shape.

━━━ Child who is the bag.
She stands behind the other child and follows his movements.

3 'Stretch out as far as you can and push the bag right out. It's heavy, so really push.' (Encourage use of all parts of the body.) If there is a human 'bag' the pusher does not have to touch the bag, which can operate around the person but with about half a metre between them. The 'bag' can move in harmony with the pusher. Of course the 'bag' and pusher can hold on to each other and move together, if you prefer. It's easier.

4 'Hold it. Freeze when you've pushed the bag out as far as you can. Feel your energy flowing right out of your body, keeping the bag out.'

5 The bag is so strong it gets heavier and heavier and begins to push you down, down, feel your energy coming in. What happens to your body?'

6 'The bag keeps pushing and pushing you. When your energy is completely in, freeze, hold it. How does it feel?'

7 Repeat from 3 to 6 several times encouraging:
a   different big and small shapes in different directions and levels;
b   the experience of different feelings of expansion and contraction.

8 Sound can be made by percussion or your voice: perhaps 'schusssh' when they get smaller and 'ahhhh' when they grow. Taped music can also be used.

Balancing

Soft Energy and Floating

1 Discuss the effect of gravity on movement. How do men in space walk differently from those on earth?

2 'Try floating a little with each step.'

3 'Make each step bigger and bigger.'

4 'Use your hands to help you. Go round or over objects such as chairs, tables.'

5 'You might float up and when you come down land on another part of your body.'

6 'Find a partner, hold on to each other and float together.'

7 'Join to make bigger groups until the whole class if floating together.'

8 Music: anything floaty, such as Paul Horn's 'Flute and Voice in the Taj Mahal', Tangerine Dream's 'Phaedra' or Beethoven's 'Moonlight Sonata'.

Hard Energy

Balancing on different parts of the body is the same as altering the centre line or axis of the body from one position to another (it can also be called shifting the weight.)

Sometimes, when the position is changed, the axis stays the same.

This can be explored by a primitive fighting sequence. A book that would give interesting back-up is *People of Kau*, by Leni Riefenstahl (William Collins and Sons Ltd, London, 1976). Pick a tribe from whatever part of the world you feel is appropriate. This can be a useful sequence with boys who find it difficult to control themselves or who are boisterous. Talk about tribes and how they make laws to suit the way they live and to give the people of the tribe barriers within which to live; how warriors need to obey the chief completely in battle or it could mean the death of the whole tribe. The warrior must be completely trustworthy and obedient.

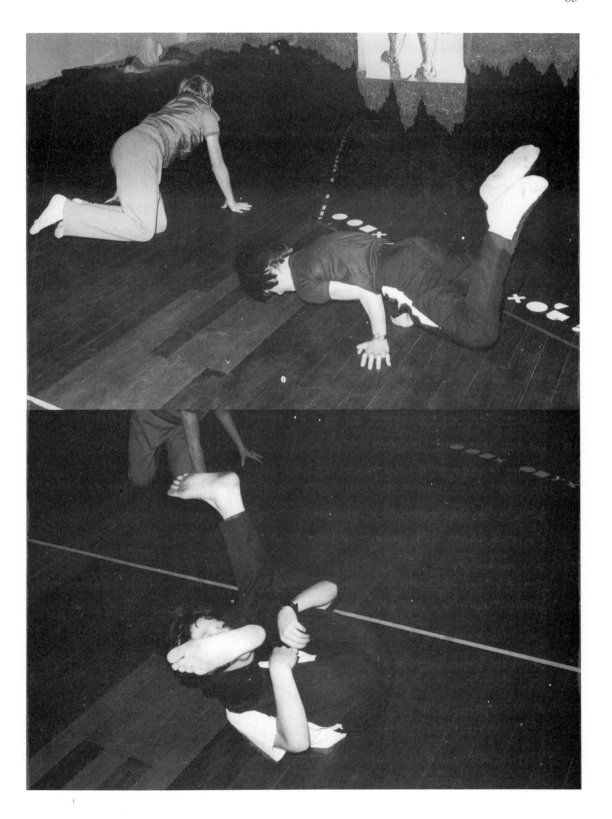

1 The teacher becomes the chief in order to direct the dance. (Later, perhaps, a child can take over.)

2 The warriors must be self-controlled and perform the dance with the necessary ferocity and strength, in order to prove their credibility as warriors.

3 The warriors line up on either side of the room, each opposite an opponent. They assume intensely fierce expressions on faces and bodies, trying to frighten their opponents across the room to gain an advantage before the battle starts. (Face paint can be daubed on by the children, however they like.)

4 The children stand strongly with weight balanced and feet wide and braced in a fighting stance. With their arms out, they look at and size up their opponents.

5 At this point a sound can come to scare the opponent. The sound comes from the stomach, not the throat, and is deep and full of energy.

6 The two opponents walk towards each other, eyeing each other. The walk is actually a slow series of balances. One leg is lifted high then pounded down on the ground. The top of the body sways from side to side as the leg is lifted (that is, changes axis). Perhaps use a sound for each balance.

7 You might like to beat a rhythm on drum or clapping sticks or call 'step and step and step' (not very authentic!). Or make up a chant to give the rhythm ('Bougar, Necker, Necker!' was one we once used for a fantasy piece like this).

8 When the two groups are about two metres away from each other, they freeze (again the chief can direct this with drum or a command in a made-up language).

9 The two opponents circle slowly around each other, looking for a moment to strike. They walk crouched, keeping eye contact all the time. The movements used for circling can be whatever the children want to do, since slow balancing will be involved somewhere.

10 One of the opponents lunges and strikes out at the other, thus shifting his centre line. (This is not pre-arranged, but spontaneous and different every time. No body contact is made).

11 The blow is aimed at a particular part of the opponent's body and the attacker, once the strike is made, holds the striking position about 10 centimetres from the opponent's body, making the position as big as possible, as in the figure below.

12 The recipient, although not actually touched, reacts to the blow by contracting the part of the body that has been 'hit', thus changing his axis too, as in the figure below.

13 The person who has been attacked recovers, changes axis, and aims a blow at a specific part of his opponent's body. His opponent then reacts and changes axis. The positions are held. (See the figure below.)

When beginning, choose topics which appeal to the background and age group of the students. They can be led into different topics later.

14   Repeat 10 and 11.

15   At this point the children can improvise an end. Although under the heading of 'balancing', this exercise involves many movements and feelings. Allow it to go in whatever direction it develops, as long as you and the children enjoy it.

Landscapes

Introduction

Landscapes have been introduced in Exercise 19 on page 62. The idea, as in 'The Wizard' is to be able to disregard the room as it is and create a new landscape using mental pictures.

This can be done in several ways:

1   A common fantasy. The class agrees beforehand about such 'facts' as 'There's a tree here.' (A spot is specifically indicated and can even be marked in some way.) The whole class agrees that they are going to create a mental picture of a tree on that spot.

2   An individual fantasy. Each child, although given the same stimulus, creates something different, as in 'The Gift', where everyone's special thing is different.

3   A common individual fantasy. The children all explore the same thing; for example, a planet. Each child's planet is different from the others'; odours, concepts, objects and form differ from child to child. They all move about the room exploring imaginary objects, but there has been no agreement beforehand about what those objects are. Thus the children are using the common space but creating individual fantasies.

Movement orientated stimuli (see Chapter 4) can be used to suggest fantasies: for example,

1   A scarf becomes the special present, as in 'The Gift'.

2   A chair can mark the place of a tree, as in 'A Walk in the Forest' (below).

3   A mask changes the space traveller into a monster, as in 'Space Journey' (below).

4   Ropes can make a pond, a house or a mountain.

A Walk in the Forest

Below is a fantasy piece in which all four ways of creating mental pictures have been used. Depending on the age group, you can do the whole thing in one lesson or one or two sections per lesson. Adjust the formal language that I have used too.

1 'Lie on the floor in your own space.' (Relaxation exercise) Have children become aware of the body on the floor and of their personal space.

2 'Change the feeling of the floor. Create a mental picture that there is grass under you. As you lie there feel the grass, smell it.'

3 'As you lie there, create a mental picture of a forest all around you. The trees, flowers, birds, insects, sky, wind, sun, etc. Create the size, shape, colour, mass, texture, smell, sound and mood of these things.' (This will depend upon the competence and age of children.)

4 'Sit up and touch the grass. What does it look, feel, smell and taste like? What temperature is it? Try different movements in the grass, (eg rolling, rubbing, sniffing) with different parts of the body.'

5 'Crawl along in the grass. Suddenly you see a beautiful flower. Reach out and touch it, all over, explore the whole shape, creating the size, colour, and mass while you do that. Smell it, not only the flower but the stem as well. How does it feel, is it strong or fragile? React to the flower, what do you do about it?' (Sometimes children will want to use this as an opportunity to destroy or mutilate. Use your discretion about whether to stop the destruction or not. I often find it best in an exercise of this nature not to comment unless the children get out of control.)

6 The children then explore other things in the forest in a similar way, creating individual common fantasies.

7 Common fantasy. Agree beforehand that the hoops lying on the ground are going to be trees. The children are asked to go round the hoops in groups. They are told that the trunk is as wide as the hoop and asked to run their hands round and over the roots of the tree. This time they are aware of each other and their tree (as opposed to creating their individual fantasies within the common space as they did in the other part of the exercise).

8 The children explore the roots, then up the trunk, (aware of size, mass, texture, smell, taste, colour and temperature). They climb the tree being aware of others and making it a group effort.

9 'Have a rest. Sit on a rock.'

10 'Explore a big pond (indicated perhaps by ropes). What happens?'

11 'Find a special sleeping place for yourself in the forest. What part of the forest is it in? What's it like?'

12 'Lie down. How do you feel?'

13 Now take the children out of the fantasy: 'The forest is fading, fading. Be

aware of your body on the floor, the forest under your body is going, feel the floor of the classroom under you.'

14 Relaxation exercise.

15 'Put out your hands, feel the floor of the classroom with them.'

16 'Sit up and look around.'

17 Do some exercises to bring the children back into present time. See Exercises 25–28 on page 66. Music and percussion sounds work well.

Additions

You could also use mask work in 'A Walk in the Forest', as follows.
1 After Step 1, when the children are 'sleeping', give some children masks of forest animals (or some other objects that represent forest animals).

2 The animals go and visit someone who has not got a mask. The animal makes a statue to show what kind of animal it is, near one or more of the sleepers.

3 The sleepers awake and relate to the animals, making a statue to show their reactions to the animals.

4 The animals make statues to show their reactions to the sleepers.

5 Free improvisation.

6 Back to sleeping places.

7 Carry on with step 13, page 90, taking the children out of the fantasy.

Comments

This type of exercise can form the basis for whatever theme you want to explore. I shall give one more example: 'Space Journey'. Generally these fantasies, which involve several different types of space follow a pattern:
1 Stillness and awareness of personal space.

2 Movement in personal space.

3 Movement through common space with personal space around them.

4 Movement through common space, aware of self and others in the space.

5 Movement through common space with personal space around them.

6 Movement in personal space.

7 Stillness in personal space.

   Not every fantasy piece you do will completely follow this formula, but keep it in mind. 'Space Journey' follows this formula.

Space Journey

1 The children lie on the floor and do relaxation exercises for awareness of body in personal space.

2 Tell the children that they are going on a journey into space. Ask them to get a mental picture of the outside of their space ship. (Use all the necessary ingredients for creating that picture — size, shape, etc. — see introduction on page 71. This stands for any mental pictures created during this fantasy.)

3 How do they get into it?

4 Now a mental picture of the inside of their space ship.

5 Where are the controls? Can they see out? How many people can they fit in the ship? Furniture? etc.

6 'When you hear the music, get up and in your space build the ship.'

7 'When you have finished, sit in your ship.'

8 Mental picture of what is needed for the journey.

9 To music put provisions into space ship. Food, etc. is taken out of the air or off a 'loading dock' and loaded in the space ship.

10 Mental image picture of your space suit.

11 (To music) 'put your suit on. Take your special outfit off the hanger and mime getting into it. Do you have shoes, gloves, a helmet? Put it on carefully.

12 'Sit at the controls, ready for count down.'

13 'Count down, blast off!'

14 'Steer the ship up away from the classroom, school, city, state, Australia, the world, until you are up in outer space.' (This can be done with a mental picture whilst the children sit in their personal spaces and work the controls of their ship, rather than moving physically round the room.)

15 'Freeze! Look out of your space ship and see what you can see.'

16 'Fly on again.'

17 'In front of you is the planet on which you are going to land. Look at it. What colour, size and shape is it?'

18 'Steer your space ship towards it and see it come closer and closer until you can land on it.'

19 'Stop the space ship, get up and go to the door (or however you get out). Freeze.'

20 'Be careful; you don't know what's out there. Slowly look out of the ship and see what your planet looks like, look all around, see if it is safe.'

21 'Whisper to yourself some of the things you can see, if you know what they are.'

22 'When I say "go", get out of your ship and begin to move around your planet. This is not Earth but your special planet, and you have a special way of moving on that planet, unlike how you would move on Earth. See what part of your body leads when you move on this planet. Go!'

23 Move and freeze alternately.

24 Explore objects on the planet as in 'A Walk in the Forest' steps 4 and 5. Encourage the children to change the whole room and the objects in it into their planet by the use of mental pictures.

25 'Can you find anything to eat? Try a few things.'

26 'Find a place on the planet where you can rest. Close your eyes. Go to sleep.'

27 Give some of the children creature masks. (It is best if masks are not seen beforehand.) They are asked to put them on, find someone without a mask (who is still asleep) and make a statue by them.

28 Space travellers (those without masks) wake up and react to creatures, making a statue to show how they feel.

29 Creatures react and make a statue.

30 Free improvisation.

31 Back to sleeping places; rest; creatures take off masks and become space travellers again.

32 'Wake up. Move around planet (don't forget special way of moving).'

33 'Collect some things you would like to take back with you.'

34 'Get into your space ship.'

35 'Take off. Leave the planet. Freeze. Look out from space and see your planet. Look at its size, shape and colour.

36 'Head for Earth.'

37 'Line your ship up over the world, over Australia, your state, your city, the school, the room, your spot in the room.'

38 'Land it.'

39 'Lie down, see and feel the space ship around you, let the picture of the space ship dissolve. Let your space suit go, all the things in the space ship go, the controls, the things you brought with you, and the furniture. Let the outside of the ship disappear.'

40 'Be aware of your body on the floor (relaxation).'

41 'Sit up, look around.'

42 Do exercises to get into present time.

Comment

If these exercises are too complex for your children, they can be adjusted. For example, 'Space Journey' for Kindergarten or Prep.:

1 The children make the shape of the ship with their hands around and above them.

2 Count down.

3 Children drive the ship.

4 Children do big floating space walks.

5   They meet a space monster and react.

6   They drive the ship home.

Stories

Movement Pieces

Using a story to make a movement piece is usually a question of stylisation and exaggeration. Below is an example of how a story can be made into a movement piece using a narrator. It will give you the general idea for adapting stories that the children make up or that you find in books. This is part of the Aboriginal legend of 'The Rainbow Serpent.' Children can suggest and try out movements until you come up with the final piece.

1   Narrator says: 'Once upon a time there were no people or animals, no trees or mountains, everything was all flat.'

    Movement: All the children lie flat on the floor.

2   Narrator says   'The Great Rainbow Serpent moved and went off to find his own people.'

    Movement: Three children under a piece of material get up from the floor and begin to move, with snake-like movements.

3   Narrator says: 'As he travelled, his great body made a big red mountain at Narradonga.'

    Movement: A child covered in a piece of red material makes the shape of a mountain when the Rainbow Serpent touchs him.

4   And so on, each piece of the story being given a movement or sequence of movements.

5   To help the children get into character do some work beforehand getting them to feel and move like the character they are going to be.

6   If there is conversation in the story the words can be replaced with gestures and facial expressions.

Dance

Another way of interpreting a story or part of a story in movement is to choose the movements that would suit the characters best then weave them into a dance which suggests the story. A narrator is not used, and perhaps the story itself is not as clear, but the children have to really look at the feelings behind the story and the types of characters involved. For example, a story about a Princess who is rude to a Frog:

1   Choose movements that suit the Frog: small shape, squatting, jumping, handspring, jumping.

Girls can be aggressive or play male roles in drama.

2   Choose movements that suit the Princess playing: skip, sway, turn, big shape.

3   Now look at the mood of the characters: the Frog is neutral then over-whelmed; the Princess is bored, then aggressive.

4   While the Frog does his small shape and jumps, show him going about his daily business, then becoming aware of the Princess, then being over-whelmed by her rudeness.

5   The Princess's floor pattern goes towards the frog in order to get his atten-tion, then away from him.

6   The whole dance could go like this:
    a   Frog does his sequence, alone, with a neutral expression, then freezes.
    b   Princess comes in and does her sequence once, bored and not noticing the Frog until the big shape at the end.
    c   Princess then begins to repeat her sequence. She skips towards the Frog and sways, with her tongue out.
    d   The Frog, affronted, gets smaller. This does not stop the Princess, so he jumps round behind her (using the squatting jump).
    e   The Princess turns and pokes the Frog, who does a handspring jump out of her way and freezes, looking hurt.
    f   The Princess makes a big shape and raises her fist, looking menacing.

   A combination of movement pieces and dance is effective too, especially for longer stories and performances.

Role Playing

Role playing has been developed as a drama technique and you will be able to find exercises on it in drama books. These can be developed into dance pieces and are most useful in enabling children to see dance as a medium with which to express their emotions.

Perhaps a story has come up in the children's morning news: 'Mum went to hospital. I stayed at home with Dad. He can't cook, so we had sandwiches for tea.'

1   The child whose news it is can play any part in the role play and get other children to play the other people in the story.

2   'Mum gets in the car.'
    Movements: Sway, small shape.

3   How did you feel? 'I felt sad.'
    Movements: Sway, small shape.

4   'Dad cooked tea.'
    Movements: Stir, chop, pour.

5 'He burnt it. He was angry.'
  Movements: Big shape (surprise), run (to stove), stamp (anger).

6 'I laughed. Dad looked funny.'
  Movements: Alternate big and small shape for laughter.

7 'Then I cried, because we had sandwiches for tea.'
  Movements: Small shape, stillness.

8 'Mum comes out tomorrow!'
  Movement: Big jump, skip, big jump.

Comment

Movements for making a role-play session into a dance must be exaggerated and stylised from everyday movements in order to look effective. The idea is not to mime the actions and make them look real, but to create a movement sequence. However if this is beyond your children or they need to work up to that level, accept and work with whatever and wherever they are.

chapter 7: relaxation

Relaxation!

Introduction

I shall not deal with relaxation in great detail in this handbook. There are details of relaxation exercises that will suit your class in books on yoga, and in relaxation manuals. A few exercises that I have found particularly useful for specific needs are given below.

Uses of Relaxation Exercises

1 To quieten and centre the children after a boisterous activity.

2 To enable the children to be aware of themselves and their personal space.

3 To enable the children to be aware of and isolate parts of their bodies.

4 To enable the children to be aware of energy and to empty their body of energy and emotion.

5 To enable the children to create mental pictures.

6 For rest.

Exercises

Relaxation for Awareness of the Body in Personal Space
(used before and after fantasy work)

a 'Lie on the floor, on your back, in your own space.'

b   'Feel your body lying on the floor.'
c   'Feel the floor under your body.'
d   'Be aware of your foot. Don't look at it or touch it, just put your mind on it, feel your toes, the sole of your foot and the the heel. What parts of your feet are touching the floor? What parts of your feet are not touching the floor? Let your foot relax and have a rest.'
e   'Now run your mind up your lower leg from the ankle to the knee. Feel your calf. What part of your calf is touching the floor? Feel it against the floor. Relax and let it rest.'
f   Go on through the other parts of the body using the same format. Ask children to be aware of the body part, see what parts are touching the floor, relax and rest it.
g   The sequence of body parts after lower leg is: knee, upper leg, buttocks, stomach, chest, (be aware of breathing), spine, shoulders, arms, hands, neck, face, back of head, then whole body again.
h   The body should then feel empty and the person aware of his/her body.
i   In creating a fantasy, the 'empty' body should be filled by the energy necessary to be whatever the fantasy demands. This should be done by the words, tone of voice and energy of the teacher. Time should be spent creating the illusion before the children begin to move (See 'The Wizard' page 75.)

Relaxation for Awareness of Different Parts of the Body

This is useful for creating body awareness before practising dance routines or basic movements.
a   'Lie on the floor on your back in your own space.'
b   'Be aware of your foot, the skin, the bones, the muscles, the blood, etc. Wiggle your foot around. Now tense it, scrunch it up really tight (with a sound). Let it go (with another sound).'
c   Go through the whole body as in the previous relaxation exercise.
d   Finish by scrunching up the whole body into a ball and 'exploding' out with a sound to lie flat on the floor.
    The two exercises above were taught to me by Jan Hamilton of Kenja Klowning.

Music

This is useful for developing a creative frame of mind.
a   'Look at a spot on the ceiling and put all the thoughts and problems of the day into that spot, with a sound.'
b   'Lie or sit comfortably in your own space.'
c   Listen to a piece of suitably relaxing and pleasant music.
d   'Allow your mind to go along with the music. See what pictures the music makes in your mind.'

Young Children

Young children have difficulty in keeping still. A game that they really like is this:

a 'Run round the room as fast as you can. Stop and freeze.'
b 'I'm going to count to six and I want you all to find a space on the floor and lie comfortably in it.' (Decrease volume as you count from one to six, so that the children get the feeling of being very quiet and still.)
c 'Now I'm coming round to look. If anyone moves any part of them, even their little finger, they are out. If you're out, you sit up and watch.
d When the children get good at this I impose a time limit: 'See who can keep still for one minute.'
e If some children always wriggle, I go and give them a massage or stroke them to help them stay still.

Comment

It is best for the children to keep their eyes open (look at a point on the ceiling) during relaxation exercises, otherwise they drift off, which is not the point of the exercises!

chapter 8: lesson formats

Introduction

1   How you, as a teacher, design your creative movement lessons is entirely up to you. You might want to give the children a taste of a variety of different aspects of movements or you might want to work through one or two aspects in detail.

2   Time can vary. You might do it all in a block of one hour per week. Or you might break it up into fifteen-minute segments throughout the week. You might want to do an hour per day or only half an hour per week.

3   Space is, of course, a limiting factor, as well as numbers of children. If you can bring in parents to help, you can 'team teach', dividing your class into groups. If you can hire the local hall to ease the pressure, then do so. Sometimes the children can divide into groups and one group works while the others watch. If all else fails, adapt as many of the exercises as you can to be done while sitting at a desk! Hand dances are excellent for this.

Ideas for Lesson Formats

Below are ideas to show different formats for lessons. Some contain many different sections, others just a couple. These are not plans for you to follow, just examples of the variety of lessons you can give.

Example A
1   Warm up.
2   Exploration of basic movements.
3   Relaxation.
4   Fantasy.

Example B

1 Warm up.
2 Exploration of basic movements.
3 Make own dance.
4 Show dances.

Example C

1 Warm up.
2 Continue dance making from previous lesson.
3 Show dances.
4 Short dance around to some music that one of the children has brought in — 'free dancing'.

Example D

1 Warm up.
2 Relaxation.
3 Exploring emotions through the basic movements.
4 Exploring emotions through masks.
5 A game of 'Tag'.

Example E

1 Warm up.
2 Relaxation.
3 Mask work exercises.
4 Mask work with audience.

Example F

(if practicing for a performance)
1 Warm up.
2 Rehearsal.
3 Quick game, relaxation or free dance.

Comments

1 Always end a lesson on a high note.
2 Warm ups need only take five or ten minutes if you want to get through a lot of other things.
3 Don't be afraid to scrap a planned lesson because events have taken the lesson in another direction.

Acknowledgements

I would like to thank and to acknowledge the help, support and information given me by the following people and organisations.

Ken Dyers, director of Kenja Communication, is a leading exponent of the use of time, space and energy. His work is unique and has greatly improved the quality of my work in schools. Ken's ideas have influenced all sections of this handbook and Chapter 2 is based on his work, from which I have developed exercises suitable for children. Much of the terminology, especially in the chapter on fantasy, is Ken's. I used it because I could neither find nor invent better terminology for the purpose.

Jan Hamilton of Kenja Klowning has enabled me to experience much of the work in this handbook as a pupil. Her approach has made me aware of the creativity that can be part of human development. Her example as a teacher has encouraged me to strive for a higher level of ethics, sensitivity and awareness of others. She has inspired in me great respect for the people whom I teach.

Helen Zigmond whose support, help and ideas contributed much to this book. Helen was responsible for encouragement and proofreading.

Margaret Gardener enabled me to begin researching and writing this book and helped me throughout the project.

Anne Fahey, who helped with printing and distribution of the first version of this handbook.
Mozelle Aaron, who shared her experience and ideas with me.
The Commonwealth Schools Commission, for providing a two-year grant to research creative dance and drama by teaching in the field, training teachers and beginning this handbook.
The teachers and children of the following schools:
Riley Street Infants' School, Surry Hills, New South Wales.
Fred Birks School for Special Purposes, Royal Alexander Hospital, Camperdown, New South Wales.
Chalmers Road School for Special Purposes, Strathfield, New South Wales.
Redfern Infants' School, Redfern, New South Wales.
Burwood Public School, Burwood, New South Wales.
Crown Street Public School, Surry Hills, New South Wales.
Nicholson Street Public School, East Balmain, New South Wales.
Newtown Public School, Sydney, New South Wales.
The Mangala Yoga Centre, Carlton, Victoria, at which I was a student.

The Drama Action Centre, Greenwich, New South Wales, at which I was a student.

Don Colantonio who took many of the photographs.

William Lee and Helena Smith, two people who have encouraged my creativity, allowed it space to grow, and taught me the determination and ability to survive that belong to our parents' generation.

All the adults and children with whom I have worked, who have taught me so much.

DATE DUE

FEB 0 3 1998			
FEB 1 6 1998			
JUL 2 1 2006			
JUL 1 1 REC'D			

GAYLORD   PRINTED IN U.S.A.